Spring Phantoms

Other Anthologies Edited by Robert Alexander

Nothing to Declare: A Guide to the Flash Sequence, ed. Robert Alexander, Eric Braun, and Debra Marquart (Buffalo: White Pine Press, 2016).

Family Portrait: American Prose Poetry, 1900–1950, ed. Robert Alexander (Buffalo: White Pine Press, 2012).

The House of Your Dream: An International Collection of Prose Poetry, ed. Robert Alexander and Dennis Maloney (Buffalo: White Pine Press, 2008).

The Talking of Hands: Unpublished Writing by New Rivers Press Authors, ed. Robert Alexander, Mark Vinz, and C. W. Truesdale (Minneapolis: New Rivers Press, 1998).

The Party Train: A Collection of North American Prose Poetry, ed. Robert Alexander, Mark Vinz, and C. W. Truesdale (Minneapolis: New Rivers Press, 1996).

Other Books by Robert Alexander

Nonfiction

The Northwest Ordinance: Constitutional Politics and the Theft of Native Land (Jefferson, NC: McFarland Books, 2017).

Five Forks: Waterloo of the Confederacy (East Lansing: Michigan State Univ. Press, 2003).

Poetry

Richmond Burning (Northfield, MN: Red Dragonfly Press, 2017).

What the Raven Said (Buffalo, NY: White Pine Press, 2006).

White Pine Sucker River: Poems 1970–1990 (Minneapolis: New Rivers Press, 1993).

Spring Phantoms

Short Prose by 19th Century
British & American Authors

Edited by Robert Alexander

With biographical sketches by Holly Iglesias

WHITE PINE PRESS / BUFFALO, NEW YORK

White Pine Press
P.O. Box 236
Buffalo, NY 14201
www.whitepine.org

Marie Alexander Poetry Series, Volume 22

Publication of this book was made possible, in part, by public funds from the New York State Council on the Arts, a State Agency.

Cover image: *Wetlands Sunrise* by Anne Kessler. Copyright © 2015 by Anne Kessler. Used with permission of the artist; "painted on ancestral Pomo lands."

Printed and bound in the United States of America.

Library of Congress Control Number: 2017946294

ISBN 978-1-945680-12-0

Contents

Alphabetical List of Authors

Spring Phantoms: A Brief Introduction

It was Edgar Allan Poe who famously said that "what we term a long poem is, in fact, merely a succession of brief ones." He based this conclusion upon the supposition that "if any literary work is too long to be read at one sitting, we must be content to dispense with the immensely important effect derivable from unity of impression." Otherwise, "the affairs of the world interfere, and every thing like totality is at once destroyed." Poe then asserted that a hundred-line poem was the maximum that could be encompassed in a "single sitting"—which when translated into prose might reasonably be considered somewhere in the neighborhood of a thousand words. With anything much longer, one's mind starts going off in all sorts of directions, and it becomes impossible to hold the entire work in one's comprehension as one does, say, an individual painting or photograph. As I have said elsewhere, reading such works of short prose "has its own peculiar charm."[1]

Some fifty years after Poe's death, Lafcadio Hearn, teaching in Japan, was introducing university students to Western literature. In the following passage, he talks about the value of what he calls a "sketch," which he considers to have "a very great future":

> By the word sketch I mean any brief study in prose which is either an actual picture of life as seen with the eyes, or of life as felt with the mind. You know that the word strictly

> means a picture lightly and quickly drawn. A sketch may be a little story, providing it keeps within the world of fact and sincere feeling. It may take the form of a dialogue between two persons, providing that the conversation recorded makes for us a complete dramatic impression. It might be a prose-monologue, inspired by the experience of some country or town. It might be only a record of something seen, but so well seen that, when recorded, it is like a water-color. In short, the sketch may take a hundred forms, a thousand forms, and it offers the widest possible range for the expression of every literary faculty.

Furthermore, Hearn continues,

> Remember that we are living in a very busy age, in which the opportunity for leisurely literary work can come to but few. No matter how rich a man may be, the new exigencies of social existence will not allow him to enjoy the patient dreamy life of the past. In a century full of hurry, where every man is expected to do more than three men would have been asked to do some fifty years ago, it is much more easy and profitable to attempt brief forms of literature than long ones. Neither will the writers of a future generation have any reason to fear the competition between short and lengthy works of literary art, for the great public, no less than the literary classes, will certainly become tired of lengthy productions; their preference will be given to works of small compass which can be read in intervals of leisure.[2]

Over the years, this sort of short prose piece has gone by various names: sketch, prose poem, vignette, and—more recently—flash fiction or nonfiction. Some of the earliest narratives that fall into this category are fables, which have been in existence since people first sat around campfires. When movable type appeared in Europe around 1500, some of the first things to find their way into print were "chapbooks," small booklets or pamphlets, which in many cases were collections of such prose shorts deriving from earlier pre-print traditions.[3] They can often be found in translations—the Psalms of the King James Bible, for example—and other sorts of short prose are scattered through English literature, such as the "meditations" of John Donne and Thomas Traherne. In my opinion, however, the first use of the prose short in English as a self-conscious literary device comes at the end of the eighteenth century, in William Blake's *Marriage of Heaven and Hell.*

Historically, the prose poem as a literary form has been far better recognized in France than in England or America. In mid-nineteenth-century Paris, Charles Baudelaire began writing pieces which he called *petits poèmes en prose* (published posthumously in 1869 as *Le Spleen de Paris*). In a letter to the editor Arsène Houssaye, Baudelaire explains that his model for these pieces was Aloysius Bertrand's *Gaspard de la nuit* (1843), with its "strangely picturesque" prose sketches, adapted to "a modern and more abstract life." "Which one of us," asks Baudelaire, "has not dreamed, in his ambitious days, of the miracle of a poetic prose . . . supple enough and jarring enough to be adapted to the soul's lyrical movements, to the undulations of reverie, to the sudden starts that consciousness takes?" In his journals, Baudelaire also acknowledges his artistic debt to Alphonse Rabbe, whose collection, *L'Album d'un pessimiste* (1836), is in part a series of melancholy little sketches. After Baudelaire, French literature is replete with prose poets.[4]

Except for Lafcadio Hearn, who mentions Baudelaire's work in "Spring Phantoms," and James Huneker, who published a translation of Baudelaire's poetry, it's an open question as to who among Anglophone writers of the nineteenth century was aware of the prose poem as practiced in France. We can assume that Oscar Wilde was, since he was fluent in the language and lived for a time in France, as did his younger contemporaries Ernest Dowson and John Millington Synge. Moreover, in 1890 the American poet Stuart Merrill, who wrote for the most part in French, published an anthology of translations, *Pastels in Prose,* which introduced the French *poème en prose* to a wider audience. In his introduction to the book, William Dean Howells speaks of the prose poem as "a peculiarly modern invention"—and he goes on to say, "I do not know the history of the French Poem in Prose, but I am sure that, as we say in our graphic slang, it has come to stay."[5]

Here, for example, is Stuart Merrill's translation of a piece from Aloysius Bertrand's *Gaspard de la nuit:*

Moonlight

At the hour that separates one day from another, when the city sleeps in silence, I awoke with a start upon a winter's night, as I heard my name pronounced by my side.

My room was half dark; the moon, clad in a vaporous robe, like a white fairy, was gazing upon my sleep and smiling at me through the windows.

A nocturnal patrol was passing in the street; a homeless dog howled in a deserted cross-way, and the cricket sang in my hearth.

Soon the noises grew fainter by degrees. The nocturnal patrol had departed, a door had been opened to the poor abandoned dog, and the cricket, weary of singing, had fallen asleep; and to me, barely rid of a dream, with eyes yet dazzled by the marvels of another world, all that surrounded me seemed a dream.

Ah, how sweet it is to awaken in the middle of the night, when the moon, that glides mysteriously to your couch, awakens you with a melancholy kiss.[6]

And here is James Huneker's translation of the piece by Baudelaire that Lafcadio Hearn refers to in "Spring Phantoms":

The Gifts of the Moon

The Moon, who is caprice itself, looked in at the window as you slept in your cradle, and said to herself: "I am well pleased with this child."

And she softly descended her stairway of clouds and

passed through the window-pane without noise. She bent over you with the supple tenderness of a mother and laid her colors upon your face. Therefrom your eyes have remained green and your cheeks extraordinarily pale. From contemplation of your visitor your eyes are so strangely wide; and she so tenderly wounded you upon the breast that you have ever kept a certain readiness to tears.

In the amplitude of her joy, the Moon filled all your chamber as with a phosphorescent air, a luminous poison; and all this living radiance thought and said: "You shall be for ever under the influence of my kiss. You shall love all that loves me and that I love: clouds, and silence, and night; the vast green sea; the unformed and multitudinous waters; the place where you are not; the lover you will never know; monstrous flowers, and perfumes that bring madness; cats that stretch themselves swooning upon the piano and lament with the sweet, hoarse voices of women.

"And you shall be loved of my lovers, courted of my courtesans. You shall be the Queen of men with green eyes, whose breasts also I have wounded in my nocturnal caress: men that love the sea, the immense green ungovernable sea; the unformed and multitudinous waters; the place where they are not; the woman they will never know; sinister flowers that seem to bear the incense of some unknown religion; perfumes that trouble the will; and all savage and voluptuous animals, images of their own folly."

And that is why I am couched at your feet, O spoiled child, beloved and accursed, seeking in all your being the reflection of that august divinity, that prophetic godmother, that poisonous nurse of all *lunatics*.[7]

However well-known the French poets were in England and America, Anglophone writers were conducting experiments for the most part very different in voice, in style, and indeed in most every quality except brevity from the French *poème en prose*. Where the French tended toward the use of traditionally "poetic" elements—moon and moonlight, in the examples above—Anglophone writers, as can be seen throughout this collection, rather emphasized the narrative possibilities inherent in prose. Most of the pieces in this book—whether "fancies," journal entries, prose poems, fables, sketches, or "impressions"—have a story to tell. Some have more commentary and embellishment, some less. But overall it is the narrative element which predominates: "I alone have lived to tell this tale"—rather than the poetic: "No one ese can tell this tale as artfully as I."

Geographically, the authors included come from all across the globe—from New England (Henry Thoreau) to New Orleans (Kate Chopin) to California (Gelett Burgess), and from South Africa (Olive Schreiner) to Australia (Richard Horne) to the Pacific islands (Robert Louis Stevenson). We can see the influence of the King James translation of the Bible throughout the century—from William Blake to Oscar Wilde to Lord Dunsany—and we can see the oral roots of the short prose sketch in the translations of Alcée Fortier, Mary Alicia Owen, and Jane and Henry Schoolcraft. We see journal entries that were published as separate, standalone pieces by various different authors, such as the little sketches by Nathaniel Hawthorne and Henry Thoreau, and one by Ralph Waldo Emerson that didn't appear in print until the twentieth century—as well as one letter, by Jourdon Anderson, so articulate that it was reprinted in several contemporary newspapers before being gathered into a collection of post–Civil War freedmen's writing. We see a leaflet by Charlotte Perkins Gilman that was apparently distributed by hand.

What I have not included here are portions of longer works taken out of context, though an argument can well be made that since any longer work is by necessity written in short stretches, there are plenty of sections of novels and nonfiction—as, for example, in Thoreau's *Walden*—that their authors probably would have considered competent to stand on their own account. Some of the pieces in this anthology announce themselves as prose poems, and some, like Kate Chopin's, as stories. Some, like those of Harriet Jacobs, are from memoirs written in short segments. There are guidebook sections and newspaper articles and a couple, by Robert Browning, of brief "schemes of poems," and at least one piece, by Elizabeth Stuart Phelps, that these days would be called a "flash essay"—but what they all have in common is brevity, most of them containing fewer than a thousand words. Some were published in authors' collected works, and some only appeared in the most evanescent of publications, such as the *Fly Leaf* of Boston, a little magazine that had a life span measured in months.

We begin with work by William Blake, who was born when the thirteen American colonies were still part of Great Britain, and we end with Edward Plunkett, Lord Dunsany, who first published at the very end of the nineteenth century, and who died in 1957, exactly two hundred years after Blake's birth. By date of first publication, the earliest work here is Blake's *Marriage of Heaven and Hell* (1790), and the latest is John Millington Synge's translations from Petrarch's sonnets (1909), which he rendered in a colloquial Irish idiom. These two writers are in a stylistic sense transitional, on the one hand leading from an earlier, more formal eighteenth century diction, and on the other hand foreshadowing the use of conversational language which characterizes Modernist literature. In a century known for the prolix, I was surprised by the variety of short prose pieces I found while poking around in the nooks and crannies of the literary attic. It's my hope that this collection, being in the end truly a mixed bag, contains something for every taste.

—R.A.

Spring Phantoms

William Blake [1757–1827][1]

from The Marriage of Heaven and Hell

A Memorable Fancy

As I was walking among the fires of hell, delighted with the enjoyments of Genius; which to Angels look like torment and insanity. I collected some of their Proverbs: thinking that as the sayings used in a nation, mark its character, so the Proverbs of Hell, shew the nature of Infernal wisdom better than any description of buildings or garments. When I came home; on the abyss of the five senses, where a flat sided steep frowns over the present world. I saw a mighty Devil folded in black clouds, hovering on the sides of the rock, with corroding fires he wrote the following sentence now perceived by the minds of men, & read by them on earth.

How do you know but ev'ry Bird that cuts the airy way,
Is an immense world of delight clos'd by your senses five?

* * *

A Memorable Fancy

The Prophets Isaiah and Ezekiel dined with me, and I asked them how they dared so roundly to assert. that God spake to them; and whether they did not think at the time, that they would be misunderstood, & so be the cause of imposition.

Isaiah answer'd. I saw no God, nor heard any, in a finite organical perception; but my senses discover'd the infinite in everything, and as I was then perswaded. & remain confirm'd; that the voice of honest indignation is the voice of God, I cared not for consequences but wrote.

Then I asked: does a firm perswasion that a thing is so, make it so?
He replied. All poets believe that it does, & in ages of imagination this firm perswasion removed mountains; but many are not capable of a firm perswasion of any thing.

Then Ezekiel said. The philosophy of the east taught the first principles of human perception some nations held one principle for the origin &

some another, we of Israel taught that the Poetic Genius (as you now call it) was the first principle and all the others merely derivative, which was the cause of our despising the Priests & Philosophers of other countries, and prophecying that all Gods would at last be proved. to originate in ours & to be the tributaries of the Poetic Genius, it was this. that our great poet King David desired so fervently & invokes so patheticly, saying by this he conquers enemies & governs kingdoms; and we so loved our God. that we cursed in his name all the deities of surrounding nations, and asserted that they had rebelled; from these opinions the vulgar came to think that all nations would at last be subject to the jews.

This said he, like all firm perswasions, is come to pass, for all nations believe the jews' code and worship the jews' god, and what greater subjection can be[.]

I heard this with some wonder, & must confess my own conviction. After dinner I ask'd Isaiah to favour the world with his lost works, he said none of equal value was lost. Ezekiel said the same of his.

I also asked Isaiah what made him go naked and barefoot three years? he answerd, the same that made our friend Diogenes the Grecian.

I then asked Ezekiel. why he eat dung, & lay so long on his right & left side? he answered. the desire of raising other men into a perception of the infinite[;] this the North American tribes practice. & is he honest who resists his genius or conscience. only for the sake of present ease or gratification?

* * *

A Memorable Fancy

I was in a Printing house in Hell & saw the method in which knowledge is transmitted from generation to generation.

In the first chamber was a Dragon-Man, clearing away the rubbish from a caves mouth; within, a number of Dragons were hollowing the cave,

In the second chamber was a Viper folding round the rock & the cave, and others adorning it with gold silver and precious stones.

In the third chamber was an Eagle with wings and feathers of air, he caused the inside of the cave to be infinite, around were numbers of Eagle like men, who built palaces in the immense cliffs.

In the fourth chamber were Lions of flaming fire raging around & melting the metals into living fluids.

In the fifth chamber were Unnam'd forms, which cast the metals into the expanse.

There they were receiv'd by Men who occupied the sixth chamber, and took the forms of books & were arranged in libraries.

Leigh Hunt [1784–1859][2]

A "Now," Descriptive of a Hot Day

Now the rosy- (and lazy-) fingered Aurora, issuing from her saffron house, calls up the moist vapours to surround her, and goes veiled with them as long as she can; till Phoebus, coming forth in his power, looks everything out of the sky, and holds sharp, uninterrupted empire from his throne of beams. Now the mower begins to make his sweeping cuts more slowly, and resorts oftener to the beer. Now the carter sleeps a-top of his load of hay, or plods with double slouch of shoulder, looking out with eyes winking under his shading hat, and with a hitch upwards of one side of his mouth. Now the little girl at her grandmother's cottage-door watches the coaches that go by, with her hand held up over her sunny forehead. Now labourers look well resting in their white shirts at the doors of rural alehouses. Now an elm is fine there, with a seat under it; and horses drink out of the trough, stretching their yearning necks with loosened collars; and the traveller calls for his glass of ale, having been without one for more than ten minutes; and his horse stands wincing at the flies, giving sharp shivers of his skin, and moving to and fro his ineffectual docked tail, and now Miss Betty Wilson, the host's daughter, comes streaming forth in a flowered gown and earrings, carrying with four of her beautiful fingers the foaming glass, for which, after the traveller has drank it, she receives with an indifferent eye, looking another way, the lawful twopence. . . . Now grasshoppers "fry," as Dryden says.* Now cattle stand in water, and ducks are envied. Now boots, and shoes, and trees by the road-side, are thick with dust; and dogs, rolling in it, after issuing out of the water, into which they have been thrown to fetch sticks, come scattering horror among the legs of the spectators. Now a fellow who finds he has three miles further to go in a pair of tight shoes is in a pretty situation. Now rooms with the sun upon them become intolerable; and the apothecary's apprentice, with a bitterness beyond aloes, thinks of the pond he used to bathe in at school. Now men with powdered heads (especially if thick) envy those that are unpowdered, and stop to wipe them up hill, with countenances that seem to expostulate with destiny. Now boys assemble round the village pump with a ladle to it, and delight to make a forbidden splash and get wet through the shoes. Now also they make suckers of leather, and bathe all day long in rivers and ponds, and make mighty fishings for "tittle-bats."** Now the bee, as he hums along, seems to be talking heavily of the heat. Now doors and brick-walls are burning to the hand: and a walled lane, with dust and broken bottles in it, near a brick-field, is a thing not to be thought of. Now a green lane, on the contrary, thick-set with hedgerow elms, and having the noise of a brook "rumbling in pebblestone,"*** is one of the pleasantest things in the world.

Now, in town, gossips talk more than ever to one another, in rooms, in doorways, and out of window, always beginning the conversation with saying that the heat is overpowering. Now blinds are let down, and doors thrown open, and flannel waistcoats left off, and cold meat preferred to hot, and wonder expressed why tea continues so refreshing, and people delight to sliver lettuces into bowls, and apprentices water doorways with tin canisters that lay several atoms of dust. Now the water-cart, jumbling along the middle of the street, and jolting the showers out of its box of water, really does something. Now fruiterers' shops and dairies look pleasant, and ices are the only things to those who can get them. Now ladies loiter in baths: and people make presents of flowers; and wine is put into ice: and the after-dinner lounger recreates his head with applications of perfumed water out of long-necked bottles. Now the lounger, who cannot resist riding his new horse, feels his boots burn him. Now buckskins are not the lawn of Cos.† Now jockeys, walking in great-coats to lose flesh, curse inwardly. Now five fat people in a stagecoach hate the sixth fat one who is coming in, and think he has no right to be so large. Now clerks in office do nothing but drink soda-water and spruce-beer, and read the newspaper. Now the old-clothesman drops his solitary cry more deeply into the areas on the hot and forsaken side of the street; and bakers look vicious; and cooks are aggravated; and the steam of a tavern-kitchen catches hold of us like the breath of Tartarus.†† Now delicate skins arc beset with gnats; and boys make their sleeping companion start up, with playing a burning-glass on his hand; and blacksmiths are super-carbonated; and cobblers in their stalls almost feel a wish to be transplanted: and butter is too easy to spread; and the dragoons wonder whether the Romans liked their helmets; and old ladies, with their lappets unpinned, walk along in a state of dilapidation;

and the servant maids are afraid they look vulgarly hot; and the author, who has a plate of strawberries brought him, finds that he has come to the end of his writing.

[*] See his translation of Virgil's *Ecologues*, ii, 13.
[**] Sticklebacks: a species of small fish.
[***] [Edmund] Spenser, *Virgil's Gnat*, 163.
[†] A kind of fine linen made in the island of Cos in the Aegean.
[††] The lowest part of Hades.

Henry R. Schoolcraft [1793–1864] and Jane Johnston Schoolcraft, trans. [1800–1843][3]

Peeta Kway, The Foam-Woman: An Ottawa Legend

There once lived a woman called Monedo Kway* on the sand mountains called "the Sleeping Bear," of Lake Michigan, who had a daughter as beautiful as she was modest and discreet. Everybody spoke of the beauty of this daughter. She was so handsome that her mother feared she would be carried off, and to prevent it she put her in a box on the lake, which was tied by a long string to a stake on the shore. Every morning the mother pulled the box ashore, and combed her daughter's long, shining hair, gave her food, and then put her out again on the lake.

One day a handsome young man chanced to come to the spot at the moment she was receiving her morning's attentions from her mother. He was struck with her beauty, and immediately went home and told his feelings to his uncle, who was a great chief and a powerful magician. "My nephew," replied the old man, "go to the mother's lodge, and sit down in a modest manner, without saying a word. You need not ask her the question. But whatever *you think* she will understand, and what *she thinks* in answer you will also understand." The young man did so. He sat down, with his head dropped in a thoughtful manner, without uttering a word. He then thought, "I wish she would give me her daughter." Very soon he understood the mother's thoughts in reply. "Give you my daughter?" thought she; "*you!* No, indeed, my daughter shall never marry you." The young man went away and reported the result to his uncle. "Woman without good sense;" said he, "who is she keeping her daughter for? Does she think she will marry the Mudjikewis?** Proud heart! we will try her magic skill, and see whether she can withstand our power." The pride and haughtiness of the mother was talked of by the spirits living on that part of the lake. They met together and determined to exert their power in humbling her. For this purpose they resolved to raise a great storm on the lake. The water began to toss and roar, and the tempest became so severe, that the string broke, and the box floated off through the straits down Lake Huron, and struck against the sandy shores at its outlet. The place where it struck was near the lodge of a superannuated old spirit called Ishkwon Daimeka, or the keeper of the gate of the lakes. He opened the box and let out the beautiful daughter, took her into his lodge, and married her.

When the mother found that her daughter had been blown off by the storm, she raised very loud cries and lamented exceedingly. This she continued to do for a long time, and would not be comforted. At length, after two or three years, the spirits had pity on her, and determined to raise another storm and bring her back. It was even a greater storm than the first; and when it began to wash away the ground and encroach on the lodge of Ishkwon Daimeka, she leaped into the box, and the waves carried her back to the very spot of her mother's lodge on the shore. Monedo Equa was overjoyed; but when she opened the box, she found that her daughter's beauty had almost all departed. However, she loved her still because she was her daughter, and now thought of the young man who had made her the offer of marriage. She sent a formal message to him, but be had altered his mind, for be knew that she had been the wife of another: "*I* marry your daughter?" said he; "*your* daughter! No, indeed! I shall never marry her."

The storm that brought her back was so strong and powerful, that it tore away a large part of the shore of the lake, and swept off Ishkwon Daimeka's lodge, the fragments of which, lodging in the straits, formed those beautiful islands which are scattered in the St. Clair and Detroit rivers. The old man himself was drowned, and his bones are buried under them. They heard him singing his songs of lamentation as he was driven off on a portion of his lodge; as if he had been called to testify his bravery and sing his war song at the stake.

I ride the waters like the winds;
No storms can blench my heart.

* Female spirit or prophetess.

** A term indicative of the heir or successor to the first place in power.

Leelinau: A Chippewa Tale

The Pukwudjininees, or fairies of Lake Superior, had one of their most noted places of residence at the great sand dunes of *Naigow Wudjoo*, called by the French *La Grandes Sables*. Here they were frequently seen in bright moonlight evenings, and the fishermen while sitting in their canoes on the lake often saw them playing their pranks, and skipping over the hills. There was a grove of pines in that vicinity called the manito wac, or Spirit wood, into which they might be seen to flee, on the approach of evening, and there is a romantic little lake on those elevated sand-hills, not far back from the Great Lake, on the shores of which their tracks could be plainly seen in the sand. These tracks were not bigger than little children's footprints, and the spirits were often seen in the act of vanishing behind the little pine-trees. They love to dance in the most lonesome places, and were always full of glee and merriment, for their little voices could be plainly heard. These little men, the pukwudjininees, are not deeply malicious, but rather delighted in mischief and freaks, and would sometimes steal away a fisherman's paddle, or come at night and pluck the hunter's feathers out of his cap in the lodge, or pilfer away some of his game, or fish. On one occasion they went so far as to entice away into their sacred grove, and carry off a chief's daughter—a small but beautiful girl, who had been always inclined to be pensive, and took her seat often in these lonesome haunts. From her baby name of *Neenizu*, my dear life, she was called Leelinau, but she never attained to much size, remaining very slender, but of the most pleasing and sylph-like features, with very bright black eyes, and little feet. Her mother often cautioned her of the danger of visiting these lonely fairy haunts, and predicted, playfully, that she would one day be carried off by the Pukwudjees, for they were very frolicsome, mischievous and full of tricks.

To divert her mind from these recluse moods and tastes, she endeavored to bring about an alliance with a neighboring forester, who, though older than herself, had the reputation of being an excellent hunter, and active man, and be had even creditably been on the war path, though he had never brought home a scalp. To these suggestions Leelinau had turned rather a deaf ear. She had imbibed ideas of a spiritual life and existence, which she fancied could only be enjoyed in the Indian elysium, and instructed as she was by the old story-tellers, she could not do otherwise than deem the light and sprightly little men who made the fairy footprints as emissaries from the *Happy Land.* For this happy land she sighed and pined. Blood, and the taking of life, she said, the Great Spirit did not approve, and it could never be agreeable to minds of pure and spiritual moulds. And she longed to go to a region where there was no weeping, no cares, and no deaths. If her parents laughed at these notions as childish, her only resource was silence, or she merely revealed her emotions in her eyes. She was capable of the deepest concealment, and locked up in her heart what she feared to utter, or uttered to deceive. This proved her ruin.

At length, after a series of conversational interviews on the subject, she announced her willingness to accede to the matrimonial proposals, and the day was fixed for this purpose. She dressed herself in the finest manner possible, putting flowers in her hair, and carrying a bunch of wild flowers, mixed with tassels of the pine-tree in her hand. One only request she made, which was to make a farewell visit to the sacred grove of the fairies, before she visited the nuptial bower. This was granted, on the evening of the proposed ceremony, while the bridegroom and his friends gathered in her father's lodge, and impatiently waited her return. But they waited in vain. Night came but Leelinau was never more seen, except by a fisherman on the lake shore, who conceived that he had seen her go off with one of the tall fairies known as the fairy of Green Pines, with green plumes nodding o'er his brows; and it is supposed that she is still roving with him over the elysian fields.

Richard H. Horne [1802–1884][4]

The Old Churchyard Tree: A Prose Poem

There is an old yew tree which stands by the wall in a dark quiet corner of the churchyard.

And a child was at play beneath its widespreading branches, one fine day in the early spring. He had his lap full of flowers, which the fields and lanes had supplied him with, and he was humming a tune to himself as he wove them into garlands.

And a little girl at play among the tombstones crept near to listen; but the boy was so intent upon his garland, that he did not hear the gentle footsteps, as they trod softly over the fresh green grass. When his work was finished, and all the flowers that were in his lap were woven together in one long wreath, he started up to measure its length upon the ground, and then he saw the little girl, as she stood with her eyes fixed upon him. He did not move or speak, but thought to himself that she looked very beautiful as she stood there with her flaxen ringlets, hanging down upon her neck. The little girl was so startled by his sudden movement, that she let fall all the flowers she had collected in her apron, and ran away as fast as she could. But the boy was older and taller than she, and soon caught her, and coaxed her to come back and play with him, and help him to make more garlands; and from that time they saw each other nearly every day, and became great friends.

Twenty years passed away. Again he was seated beneath the old yew tree in the churchyard.

It was summer now; bright, beautiful summer, with the birds singing, and the flowers covering the ground, and scenting the air with their perfume.

But he was not alone now, nor did the little girl steal near on tiptoe, fearful of being heard. She was seated by his side, and his arm was round her, and she looked up into his face, and smiled as she whispered: "The first evening of our lives we were ever together was passed here: we will spend the first evening of our wedded life in the same quiet, happy place." And he drew her closer to him as she spoke.

The summer is gone; and the autumn; and twenty more summers and autumns have passed away since that evening, in the old churchyard.

A young man, on a bright moonlight night, comes reeling through the little white gate, and stumbling over the graves. He shouts and he sings, and is presently followed by others like unto himself or worse. So, they all laugh at the dark solemn head of the yew tree, and throw stones up at the place where the moon has silvered the boughs.

Those same boughs are again silvered by the moon, and they droop over his mother's grave. There is a little stone which bears this inscription:—

"Her Heart Brake in Silence."

But the silence of the churchyard is now broken by a voice—not of the youth—nor a voice of laughter and ribaldry.

"My son!—dost thou see this grave? and dost thou read the record in anguish, whereof may come repentance?"

"Of what should I repent?" answers the son; and why should my young ambition for fame relax in its strength because my mother was old and weak?"

"Is this indeed our son?" says the father, bending in agony over the grave of his beloved.

"I can well believe I am not;" exclaimeth the youth. "It is well that you have brought me here to say so. Our natures are unlike; our courses must be opposite. Your way lieth here—mine yonder!"

So the son left the father kneeling by the grave.

Again a few years are passed. It is winter, with a roaring wind and a thick gray fog. The graves in the Church-yard are covered with snow, and there are great icicles in the Church-porch. The wind now carries a swathe of snow along the tops of the graves, as though the "sheeted dead" were at some melancholy play; and hark! the icicles fall with a crash and jingle, like a solemn mockery of the echo of the unseemly mirth of one who is now coming to his final rest.

There are two graves near the old yew tree; and the grass has over grown them. A third is close by; and the dark earth at each side has just been thrown up. The bearers come; with a heavy pace they move along; the coffin heaveth up and down, as they step over the intervening graves.

Grief and old age had seized upon the father, and worn out his life; and premature decay soon seized upon the son, and gnawed away his vain ambition, and his useless strength, till he prayed to be borne, not the way yonder that was most opposite to his father and his mother, but even the same way they had gone—the way which leads to the Old Churchyard Tree.

Ralph Waldo Emerson [1803–1882][5]

Woods: A Prose Sonnet

Wise are ye, 0 ancient woods! Wiser than man. Whoso goeth in your paths or into your thickets where no paths are, readeth the same cheerful lesson whether he be a young child or a hundred years old. Comes he in good fortune or bad, ye say the same things, & from age to age. Ever the needles of the pine grow & fall, the acorns on the oak, the maples redden in autumn, & all times of the year the ground pine & the pyrola bud & root under foot. What is called fortune & what is called Time by men—ye know them not. Men have not language to describe one moment of your eternal life. This I would ask of you, 0 sacred woods, when ye shall next give me somewhat to say, give me also the tune wherein to say it. Give me a tune of your own like your winds or rains or brooks or birds; for the songs of men grow old when they have been often repeated, but yours, though a man have heard them for seventy years, are never the same, but always new, like time itself, or like love.

Nathaniel Hawthorne [1804–1864][6]

from Sketches from Memory

An Afternoon Scene

There had not been a more delicious afternoon than this, in all the train of summer—the air being a sunny perfume, made up of balm and warmth and gentle brightness. The oak and walnut trees, over my head, retained their deep masses of foliage, and the grass, though for months the pasturage of stray cattle, had been revived with the freshness of early June, by the autumnal rains of the preceding week. The garb of Autumn indeed resembled that of Spring. Dandelions and buttercups were sprinkled along the roadside, like drops of brightest gold in greenest grass; and a star-shaped little flower, with a golden centre. In a rocky spot, and rooted under the stone-wall, there was one wild rose-bush, bearing three roses, very faintly tinted, but blessed with a spicy fragrance. The same tokens would have announced that the year was brightening into the glow of Summer. There were violets, too, though few and pale ones. But the breath of September was diffused through the mild air, whenever a little breeze shook out the latent coolness.

A Night Scene

The steamboat in which I was a passenger for Detroit, had put into the mouth of a small river, where the greater part of the night would be spent in repairing some damages of the machinery. As the evening was warm, though cloudy and very dark, I stood on deck, watching a scene that would not have attracted a second glance in the day-time, but became picturesque by the magic of strong light and deep shade. Some wild Irishmen were replenishing our stock of wood, and had kindled a great fire on the bank, to illuminate their labors. It was composed of large logs and dry brushwood, heaped together with careless profusion, blazing fiercely, spouting showers of sparks into the darkness, and gleaming wide over lake Erie—a beacon for perplexed voyagers, leagues from land. All around and above the furnace, there was total obscurity. No trees, or other objects, caught and reflected any portion of the brightness, which thus wasted itself in the immense void of night, as if it quivered from the expiring embers of the world, after the final conflagration. But the Irishmen were continually emerging from the dense gloom, passing through the lurid glow, and vanishing into the gloom on the other side. Sometimes a whole figure would be made visible, by the shirt-sleeves and light-colored dress; others were but half seen, like imperfect creatures; many flitted, shadow-like, along the skirts of darkness, tempting fancy to a vain pursuit; and often, a face alone was reddened by the fire, and stared strangely distinct, with no traces of a body. In short, these wild Irish, distorted and exaggerated by the blaze, now lost in deep shadow, now bursting into sudden splendor, and now struggling between light and darkness, formed a picture which might have been transferred, almost unaltered, to a tale of the supernatural. As they all carried lanterns of wood, and often flung sticks upon the fire, the least imaginative spectator would at once compare them to devils, condemned to keep alive the flame of their own torment.

from The American Notebooks

Salem, August 31, 1836.—A walk, yesterday, down to the shore, near the hospital. Standing on the old grassy battery, that forms a semicircle, and looking seaward. The sun not a great way above the horizon, yet so far as to give a very golden brightness, when it shone out. Clouds in the vicinity of the sun, and nearly all the rest of the sky covered with clouds in masses, not a gray uniformity of cloud. A fresh breeze blowing from land seaward. If it had been blowing from the sea, it would have raised it in heavy billows, and caused it to dash high against the rocks. But now its surface was not all commoved with billows; there was only roughness enough to take off the gleam, and give it the aspect of iron after cooling. The clouds above added to the black appearance. A few sea-birds were flitting over the water, only visible at moments, when they turned their white bosoms towards me,—as if they were then first created. The sunshine had a singular effect. The clouds would interpose in such a manner that some objects were shaded from it, while others were strongly illuminated. Some of the islands lay in the shade, dark and gloomy, while others were bright and favored spots. The white light-house was sometimes very cheerfully marked. There was a schooner about a mile from the shore, at anchor, laden apparently with lumber. The sea all about her had the black, iron aspect which I have described; but the vessel herself was alight. Hull, masts, and spars were all gilded, and the rigging was made of golden threads. A small white streak of foam breaking around the bows, which were towards the wind. The shadowiness of the clouds overhead made the effect of the sunlight strange, where it fell.

Autumnal Characteristics

In sunny spots of woodland, boys are gathering walnuts, and shouting to one another from among the yellow foliage. There is something in the atmosphere of these warm autumnal afternoons, that gives a peculiar effect to laughter and joyous voices—it makes them far more elastic and gladsome than at other seasons. Grasshoppers, flies, and winged insects of all sorts, are more abundant now, in the middle of October, than I have seen them at any other season. Yellow butterflies flutter about in the sunshine, singly, or by pairs; but they seem to fly more feebly than in summer, and are blown out of their course by the stirring of every breeze. The crickets begin to sing early in the afternoon; and sometimes a locust may be heard. In sheltered nooks and hollows, where there is sunshine but no wind, the buzz of the many insects, congregated there, is an indescribably pleasant and cheerful sound. What a pity, that the frosty night will so soon stop their music.

Edgar Allan Poe [1809–1849][7]

Shadow—A Parable

> Yea! though I walk through the valley of the *Shadow* . . .
> —Psalm of David

Ye who read are still among the living: but I who write shall have long since gone my way into the region of shadows. For indeed strange things shall happen, and secret things be known, and many centuries shall pass away, ere these memorials be seen of men. And, when seen, there will be some to disbelieve, and some to doubt, and yet a few who will find much to ponder upon in the characters here graven with a stylus of iron.

The year had been a year of terror, and of feelings more intense than terror for which there is no name upon the earth. For many prodigies and signs had taken place, and far and wide, over sea and land, the black wings of the Pestilence were spread abroad. To those, nevertheless, cunning in the stars, it was not unknown that the heavens wore an aspect of ill; and to me, the Greek Oinos, among others, it was evident that now had arrived the alternation of that seven hundred and ninety-fourth year when, at the entrance of Aries, the planet Jupiter is conjoined with the red ring of the terrible Saturnus. The peculiar spirit of the skies; if I mistake not greatly, made itself manifest, not only in the physical orb of the earth, but in the souls, imaginations, and meditations of mankind.

Over some flasks of the red Chian wine, within the walls of a noble hall, in a dim city called Ptolemais, we sat, at night, a company of seven. And to our chamber there was no entrance save by a lofty door of brass: and the door was fashioned by the artisan Corinnos, and, being of rare workmanship, was fastened from within. Black draperies, likewise, in the gloomy room, shut out from our view the moon, the lurid stars, and the peopleless streets—but the boding and the memory of Evil, they would not be so excluded. There were things around us and about of which I can render no distinct account—things material and spiritual—heaviness in the atmosphere—a sense of suffocation—anxiety—and, above all, that terrible state of existence which the nervous experience when the senses are keenly living and awake, and meanwhile the powers of thought lie dormant. A dead weight hung upon us. It hung upon our limbs—upon the household furniture—upon the goblets from which we drank; and all things were depressed, and borne down thereby—all things save only the flames of the seven iron lamps which illumined our revel. Up-rearing themselves in tall slender lines of light, they thus remained burning all pallid and motionless; and in the mirror which their lustre formed upon the round table of ebony at which we sat, each of us there assembled beheld the pallor of his own countenance, and the unquiet glare in the downcast eyes of his companions. Yet we laughed and were merry in our proper way—which was hysterical; and sang the songs of Anacreon—which are madness; and drank deeply—although the purple wine reminded us of blood. For there was yet another tenant of our chamber in the person of young Zoilus. Dead, and at full length he lay, enshrouded;—the genius and the demon of the scene. Alas! he bore no portion in our mirth, save that his countenance, distorted with the plague, and his eyes in which Death had but half extinguished the fire of the pestilence, seemed to take such interest in our merriment as the dead may haply take in the merriment of those who are to die. But although I, Oinos, felt that the eyes of the departed were upon me, still I forced myself not to perceive the bitterness of their expression, and, gazing down steadily into the depths of the ebony mirror, sang with a loud and sonorous voice the songs of the son of Teios. But gradually my songs they ceased, and their echoes, rolling afar off among the sable draperies of the chamber, became weak, and undistinguishable, and so faded away. And lo! from among those sable draperies where the sounds of the song departed, there came forth a dark and undefined shadow—a shadow such as the moon, when low in heaven, might fashion from the figure of a man: but it was the shadow neither of man, nor of God, nor of any familiar thing. And quivering awhile among the draperies of the room, it at length rested in full view upon the surface of the door of brass. But the shadow was vague, and formless, and indefinite, and was the shadow neither of man nor God—neither God of Greece, nor God of Chaldea, not any Egyptian God. And the shadow rested upon the brazen doorway, and under the arch of the entablature of the door, and moved not, nor spoke any word, but there became stationary and remained. And the door whereupon the shadow rested was, if I remember aright, over against the feet of the young Zoilus enshrouded. But we, the seven there assembled, having seen the shadow as it came out from among the draperies, dared not steadily behold it, but cast down our eyes, and gazed continually into the depths of the mirror of ebony. And at length I, Oinos, speaking some low words, demanded of the shadow its dwelling and its appellation. And the shadow answered, "I am SHADOW , and my dwelling is near to the Catacombs of Ptolemais, and hard by those dim plains of Helusion which border upon the foul Charonian canal." And then did we, the seven, start from our seats in horror, and stand trembling, and shuddering, and aghast: for the tones in the voice of the shadow were not the tones of any one being, but of a multitude of beings, and, varying in their cadences from syllable to syllable, fell duskily upon our ears in the well remembered and familiar accents of many thousand departed friends.

Harriet Jacobs [1813–1897][8]

from Incidents in the Life of a Slave Girl

The Slaves' New Year's Day

Dr. Flint owned a fine residence in town, several farms, and about fifty slaves, besides hiring a number by the year.

Hiring-day at the south takes place on the 1st of January. On the 2nd, the slaves are expected to go to their new masters. On a farm, they work until the corn and cotton are laid. They then have two holidays. Some masters give them a good dinner under the trees. This over, they work until Christmas eve. If no heavy charges are meantime brought against them, they are given four or five holidays, whichever the master or overseer may think proper. Then comes New Year's eve; and they gather together their little alls, or more properly speaking, their little nothings, and wait anxiously for the dawning of day. At the appointed hour the grounds are thronged with men, women, and children, waiting, like criminals, to hear their doom pronounced. The slave is sure to know who is the most humane, or cruel master, within forty miles of him.

It is easy to find out, on that day, who clothes and feeds his slaves well; for he is surrounded by a crowd, begging, "Please, massa, hire me this year. I will work *very* hard, massa."

If a slave is unwilling to go with his new master, he is whipped, or locked up in jail, until he consents to go, and promises not to run away during the year. Should he chance to change his mind, thinking it justifiable to violate an extorted promise, woe unto him if he is caught! The whip is used till the blood flows at his feet; and his stiffened limbs are put in chains, to be dragged in the field for days and days!

If he lives until the next year, perhaps the same man will hire him again, without even giving him an opportunity of going to the hiring-ground. After those for hire are disposed of, those for sale are called up.

O, you happy free women, contrast *your* New Year's day with that of the poor bond-woman! With you it is a pleasant season, and the light of the day is blessed. Friendly wishes meet you everywhere, and gifts are showered upon you. Even hearts that have been estranged from you soften at this season, and lips that have been silent echo back, "I wish you a happy New Year." Children bring their little offerings, and raise their rosy lips for a caress. They are your own, and no hand but that of death can take them from you.

But to the slave mother New Year's day comes laden with peculiar sorrows. She sits on her cold cabin floor, watching the children who may all be torn from her the next morning; and often does she wish that she and they might die before the day dawns. She may be an ignorant creature, degraded by the system that has brutalized her from childhood; but she has a mother's instincts, and is capable of feeling a mother's agonies.

On one of these sale days, I saw a mother lead seven children to the auction-block. She knew that *some* of them would be taken from her; but they took *all*. The children were sold to a slave-trader, and their mother was bought by a man in her own town. Before night her children were all far away. She begged the trader to tell her where he intended to take them; this he refused to do. How *could* he, when he knew he would sell them, one by one, wherever he could command the highest price? I met that mother in the street, and her wild, haggard face lives to-day in my mind. She wrung her hands in anguish, and exclaimed, "Gone! All gone! Why *don't* God kill me?" I had no words wherewith to comfort her. Instances of this kind are of daily, yea, of hourly occurrence.

Slaveholders have a method, peculiar to their institution, of getting rid of *old* slaves, whose lives have been worn out in their service. I knew an old woman, who for seventy years faithfully served her master. She had become almost helpless, from hard labor and disease. Her owners moved to Alabama, and the old black woman was left to be sold to anybody who would give twenty dollars for her.

What Slaves Are Taught to Think of the North

Slaveholders pride themselves upon being honorable men; but if you were to hear the enormous lies they tell their slaves, you would have small respect for their veracity. I have spoken plain English. Pardon me. I cannot use a milder term. When they visit the north, and return home, they tell their slaves of the runaways they have seen, and describe them to be in the most deplorable condition. A slaveholder once told me that he had seen a runaway friend of mine in New York, and that she besought him to take her back to her master, for she was literally dying of starvation; that many days she had only one cold potato to eat, and at other times could get nothing at all. He said he refused to take her, because he knew her master would not thank him for bringing such a miserable wretch to his house. He ended by saying to me, "This is the punishment she brought on herself for running away from a kind master."

This whole story was false. I afterwards stayed with that friend in New York, and found her in comfortable circumstances. She had never thought of such a thing as wishing to go back to slavery. Many of the slaves believe such stories, and think it is not worthwhile to exchange slavery for such a hard kind of freedom. It is difficult to persuade such that freedom could make them useful men, and enable them to protect their wives and children. If those heathen in our Christian land had as much teaching as some Hindoos, they would think otherwise. They would know that liberty is more valuable than life. They would begin to understand their own capabilities, and exert themselves to become men and women.

But while the Free States sustain a law which hurls fugitives back into slavery, how can the slaves resolve to become men? There are some who strive to protect wives and daughters from the insults of their masters; but those who have such sentiments have had advantages above the general mass of slaves. They have been partially civilized and Christianized by favorable circumstances. Some are bold enough to *utter* such sentiments to their masters. O, that there were more of them!

Some poor creatures have been so brutalized by the lash that they will sneak out of the way to give their masters free access to their wives and daughters. Do you think this proves the black man to belong to an inferior order of beings? What would *you* be, if you had been born and brought up a slave, with generations of slaves for ancestors? I admit that the black man *is* inferior. But what is it that makes him so? It is the ignorance in which white men compel him to live; it is the torturing whip that lashes manhood out of him; it is the fierce bloodhounds of the South, and the scarcely less cruel human bloodhounds of the north, who enforce the Fugitive Slave Law. *They* do the work.

Southern gentlemen indulge in the most contemptuous expressions about the Yankees, while they, on their part, consent to do the vilest work for them, such as the ferocious bloodhounds and the despised negro hunters are employed to do at home. When southerners go to the north, they are proud to do them honor; but the northern man is not welcome south of Mason and Dixon's line, unless he suppresses every thought and feeling at variance with their "peculiar institution." Nor is it enough to be silent. The masters are not pleased, unless they obtain a greater degree of subservience than that; and they are generally accommodated. Do they respect the northerner for this? I trow not. Even the slaves despise "a northern man with southern principles;" and that is the class they generally see. When northerners go to the south to reside, they prove very apt scholars. They soon imbibe the sentiments and disposition of their neighbors, and generally go beyond their teachers. Of the two, they are proverbially the hardest masters.

They seem to satisfy their consciences with the doctrine that God created the Africans to be slaves. What a libel upon the heavenly Father, who "made of one blood all nations of men!" And then who *are* Africans? Who can measure the amount of Anglo-Saxon blood coursing in the veins of American slaves?

I have spoken of the pains slaveholders take to give their slaves a bad opinion of the north; but, notwithstanding this, intelligent slaves are aware that they have many friends in the Free States. Even the most ignorant have some confused notions about it. They knew that I could read; and I was often asked if I had seen any thing in the newspapers about white folks over in the big north, who were trying to get their freedom for them. Some believe that the abolitionists have already made them free, and that it is established by law, but that their masters prevent the law from going into effect. One woman begged me to get a newspaper and read it over. She said her husband told her that the black people had sent word to the queen of 'Merica that they were all slave; that she didn't believe it, and went to Washington city to see the President about it. They quarreled; she drew her sword upon him, and swore that he should help her to make them all free.

That poor, ignorant woman thought that America was governed by a Queen, to whom the President was subordinate. I wish the President was subordinate to Queen Justice.

Christmas Festivities

Christmas was approaching. Grandmother brought me materials, and I busied myself making some new garments and little playthings for my children.

Were it not that hiring day is near at hand, and many families are fearfully looking forward to the probability of separation in a few days, Christmas might be a happy season for the poor slaves. Even slave mothers try to gladden the hearts of their little ones on that occasion. Benny and Ellen had their Christmas stockings filled. Their imprisoned mother could not have the privilege of witnessing their surprise and joy. But I had the pleasure of peeping at them as they went into the street with their new suits on. I heard Benny ask a little playmate whether Santa Claus brought him any thing. "Yes," replied the boy; "but Santa Claus ain't a real man. It's the children's mothers that put things into the stockings." "No, that can't be," replied Benny, "for Santa Claus brought Ellen and me these new clothes, and my mother has been gone this long time."

How I longed to tell him that his mother made those garments, and that many a tear fell on them while she worked!

Every child rises early on Christmas morning to see the Johnkannaus. Without them, Christmas would be shorn of its greatest attraction. They consist of companies of slaves from the plantations, generally of the lower class. Two athletic men, in calico wrappers, have a net thrown over them, covered with all manner of bright-colored stripes. Cows' tails are fastened to their backs, and their heads are decorated with horns. A box, covered with sheepskin, is called the gumbo box. A dozen beat on this, while others strike triangles and jawbones, to which bands of dancers keep time. For a month previous they are composing songs, which are sung on this occasion. These companies, of a hundred each, turn out early in the morning, and are allowed to go round till twelve o'clock, begging for contributions. Not a door is left unvisited where there is the least chance of obtaining a penny or a glass of rum. They do not drink while they are out, but carry the rum home in jugs, to have a carousal. These Christmas donations frequently amount to twenty or thirty dollars. It is seldom that any white man or child refuses to give them a trifle. If he does, they regale his ears with the following song:—

"Poor massa, so dey say;
Down in de heel, so dey say;
Got no money, so dey say;
Not one shillin, so dey say;
God A'mighty bress you, so dey say."

Christmas is a day of feasting, both with white and colored people. Slaves, who are lucky enough to have a few shillings, are sure to spend them for good eating; and many a turkey and pig is captured, without saying, "By your leave, sir." Those who cannot obtain these, cook a 'possum, or a raccoon, from which savory dishes can be made. My grandmother raised poultry and pigs for sale; and it was her established custom to have both a turkey and a pig roasted for Christmas dinner.

On this occasion, I was warned to keep extremely quiet, because two guests had been invited. One was the town constable, and the other was a free colored man, who tried to pass himself off for white, and who was always ready to do any mean work for the sake of currying favor with white people. My grandmother had a motive for inviting them. She managed to take them all over the house. All the rooms on the lower floor were thrown open for them to pass in and out; and after dinner, they were invited up stairs to look at a fine mocking bird my uncle had just brought home. There, too, the rooms were all thrown open, that they might look in. When I heard them talking on the piazza, my heart almost stood still. I knew this colored man had spent many nights hunting for me. Every body knew he had the blood of a slave father in his veins; but for the sake of passing himself off for white, be was ready to kiss the slaveholders' feet. How I despised him! As for the constable, he wore no false colors. The duties of his office were despicable, but he was superior to his companion, inasmuch as he did not pretend to be what be was not. Any white man, who could raise money enough to buy a slave, would have considered himself degraded by being a constable; but the office enabled its possessor to exercise authority. If he found any slave out after nine o'clock, he could whip him as much as he liked; and that was a privilege to be coveted. When the guests were ready to depart, my grandmother gave each of them some of her nice pudding, as a present for their wives. Through my peep-hole I saw them go out of the gate, and I was glad when it closed after them. So passed the first Christmas in my den.

Prejudice against Color

It was a relief to my mind to see preparations for leaving the city. We went to Albany in the steamboat Knickerbocker. When the gong sounded for tea,

Mrs. Bruce said, "Linda, it is late, and you and baby had better come to the table with me." I replied, "I know it is time baby had her supper, but I had rather not go with you, if you please. I am afraid of being insulted." "O no, not if you are with *me*," she said. I saw several white nurses go with their ladies, and I ventured to do the same. We were at the extreme end of the table. I was no sooner seated, than a gruff voice said, "Get up! You know you are not allowed to sit here." I looked up, and, to my astonishment and indignation, saw that the speaker was a colored man. If his office required him to enforce the by-laws of the boat, he might, at least, have done it politely. I replied, "I shall not get up, unless the captain comes and takes me up." No cup of tea was offered me, but Mrs. Bruce handed me hers and called for another. I looked to see whether the other nurses were treated in a similar manner. They were all properly waited on.

Next morning, when we stopped at Troy for breakfast, every body was making a rush for the table. Mrs. Bruce said, "Take my arm, Linda, and we'll go in together." The landlord heard her, and said, "Madam, will you allow your nurse and baby to take breakfast with my family?" I knew this was to be attributed to my complexion; but he spoke courteously, and therefore I did not mind it.

At Saratoga we found the United States Hotel crowded, and Mr. Bruce took one of the cottages belonging to the hotel. I had thought, with gladness, of going to the quiet of the country, where I should meet few people, but here I found myself in the midst of a swarm of Southerners. I looked round me with fear and trembling, dreading to see some one who would recognize me. I was rejoiced to find that we were to stay but a short time.

We soon returned to New York, to make arrangements for spending the remainder of the summer at Rockaway. While the laundress was putting the clothes in order, I took an opportunity to go over to Brooklyn to see Ellen. I met her going to a grocery store, and the first words she said, were, "O, mother, don't go to Mrs. Hobbs's. Her brother, Mr. Thorne, has come from the south, and maybe he'll tell where you are." I accepted the warning. I told her I was going away with Mrs. Bruce the next day, and would try to see her when I came back.

Being in servitude to the Anglo-Saxon race, I was not put into a "Jim Crow car," on our way to Rockaway, neither was I invited to ride through the streets on the top of trunks in a truck; but every where I found the same manifestations of that cruel prejudice, which so discourages the feelings, and represses the energies of the colored people. We reached Rockaway before dark, and put up at the Pavilion—a large hotel, beautifully situated by the seaside—a great resort of the fashionable world. Thirty or forty nurses were there, of a great variety of nations. Some of the ladies had colored waiting-maids and coachmen, but I was the only nurse tinged with the blood of Africa. When the tea bell rang, I took little Mary and followed the other nurses. Supper was served in a long hall. A young man, who had the ordering of things, took the circuit of the table two or three times, and finally pointed me to a seat at the lower end of it. As there was but one chair, I sat down and took the child in my lap. Whereupon the young man came to me and said, in the blandest manner possible, "Will you please to seat the little girl in the chair, and stand behind it and feed her? After they have done, you will be shown to the kitchen, where you will have a good supper."

This was the climax! I found it hard to preserve my self-control, when I looked round, and saw women who were nurses, as I was, and only one shade lighter in complexion, eyeing me with a defiant look, as if my presence were a contamination. However, I said nothing. I quietly took the child in my arms, went to our room, and refused to go to the table again. Mr. Bruce ordered meals to be sent to the room for little Mary and I. This answered for a few days; but the waiters of the establishment were white, and they soon began to complain, saying they were not hired to wait on negroes. The landlord requested Mr. Bruce to send me down to my meals, because his servants rebelled against bringing them up, and the colored servants of other boarders were dissatisfied because all were not treated alike.

My answer was that the colored servants ought to be dissatisfied with *themselves,* for not having too much self-respect to submit to such treatment; that there was no difference in the price of board for colored and white servants, and there was no justification for difference of treatment. I stayed a month after this, and finding I was resolved to stand up for my rights, they concluded to treat me well. Let every colored man and woman do this, and eventually we shall cease to be trampled under foot by our oppressors.

Henry David Thoreau [1817–1862][9]

from THE JOURNAL

Aug. 18 [1853]. Rain again.

P.M.—To Great Fields.

Many leaves of the cultivated cherry are turned yellow, and a very *few* leaves of the elm have fallen,—the dead or prematurely ripe. The abundant and repeated rains since this month came in have made the last fortnight and more seem like a rainy season in the tropics,—warm, still copious rains falling straight down, contrasting with the cold, driving spring rains. Now again I am caught in a heavy shower in Moore's pitch pines on edge of Great Fields, and am obliged to stand crouching under my umbrella till the drops turn to streams, which find their way through my umbrella, and the path up the hillside is all afloat, a succession of puddles at different levels, each bounded by a ridge of dead pine-needles. An Irishman, getting out stumps and roots in Moore's Swamp, at first squatted behind a wood-pile, but, being wet to his skin, now stands up and moves about for warmth. Melons crack open before they are sweet. Is not that variety of the ambrosia going to seed by Brown's bars in Sleepy Hollow the *heterophylla*?[*] with short, pyramidal purplish spikes and dark-green entire lanceolate leaves above.

What means this sense of lateness that so comes over one now—as if the rest of the year were downhill, and if we had not performed anything before, we should not now? The season of flowers or of promise may be said to be over, and now is the season of fruits; but where is our fruit? The night of the year is approaching. What have we done with our talent? All nature prompts and reproves us. How early in the year it begins to be late! The sound of the crickets, even in the spring, makes our hearts beat with its awful reproof, while it encourages with its seasonable warning. It matters not by how little we have fallen behind; it seems irretrievably late. The year is full of warnings of its shortness, as is life. The sound of so many insects and the sight of so many flowers affect us so—the creak of the cricket and the sight of the prunella and autumnal dandelion. They say, "For the night cometh in which no man may work."

[*] No, one form of the common [HDT]

September 9th, 1857.
To the woods for white-pine cones. Very few trees bear any, and they are on their tops. I can easily manage small trees, fifteen or twenty feet high, climbing till I can reach the dangling green pickle-like fruit with my right hand, while I hold to the main stem with my left; but I am in a pickle when I get one. The cones are now all flowing with pitch, and my hands are soon so covered with it that I cannot easily cast down my booty when I would, it sticks to my fingers so; and when I get down at last and have picked them up, I cannot touch my basket with such hands but carry it on my arm, nor can I pick up my coat which I have taken off unless with my teeth—or else I kick it up and catch it on my arm. Thus I go from tree to tree, rubbing my hands from time to time in brooks and mudholes in the hope of finding something that will remove pitch, as grease does, but in vain. It is the stickiest work I ever did; yet I stick to it. I do not see how the squirrels that gnaw them off and then open them, scale by scale, keep their paws and whiskers clean. They must possess some remedy for pitch that we know nothing of, for they can touch it and not be defiled. What would I not give for the recipe! How fast I could collect cones if I could only contract with a family of squirrels to cut them off for me!—or what if I had a pair of shears eighty feet long and a derrick to wield them with!

from Walking

We hug the earth, how rarely we mount! Methinks we might elevate ourselves a little more. We might climb a tree, at least. I found my account in climbing a tree once. It was a tall white pine, on the top of a hill; and though I got well pitched, I was well paid for it, for I discovered new mountains in the horizon which I had never seen before,—so much more of the earth and the heavens. I might have walked about the foot of the tree for three-score years and ten, and yet I certainly should never have seen them. But, above all, I discovered around me,—it was near the end of June,—on the ends of the topmost branches only, a few minute and delicate red cone-like blossoms, the fertile flower of the white pine looking heavenward. I carried straightway to the village the topmost spire, and showed it to stranger jurymen who walked the streets,—for it was court-week,—and to farmers and lumber-dealers and wood-choppers and hunters, and not one had ever seen the like before, but they wondered as at a star dropped down. Tell of ancient architects finishing their works on the tops of columns as perfectly as on the lower and more visible parts! Nature has from the first expanded the minute blossoms of the forest only toward the heavens, above men's heads and unobserved by them. We see only the flowers that are under our feet in the meadows. The pines have developed their delicate blossoms on the highest twigs of the wood every summer for ages, as well over the heads of Nature's red children as of her white ones; yet scarcely a farmer or hunter in the land has ever seen them.

Above all, we cannot afford not to live in the present. He is blessed over all mortals who loses no moment of the passing life in remembering the past. Unless our philosophy hears the cock crow in every barn-yard within our horizon, it is belated. That sound commonly reminds us that we are growing rusty and antique in our employments and habits of thought. His philosophy comes down to a more recent time than ours. There is something suggested by it that is a newer testament,—the gospel according to this moment. He has not fallen astern; he has got up early, and kept up early, and to be where he is to be in season, in the foremost rank of time. It is an expression of the heath and soundness of Nature, a brag for all the world,—healthiness as of a spring burst forth, a new fountain of the Muses, to celebrate this last instant of time. Where he lives no fugitive slave laws are passed. Who has not betrayed his master many times since last he heard that note?

The merit of this bird's strain is in its freedom from all plaintiveness. The singer can easily move us to tears or to laughter, but where is he who can excite in us a pure morning joy? When, in doleful dumps, breaking the awful stillness of our wooden sidewalk on a Sunday, or, perchance, a watcher in the house of mourning, I hear a cockerel crow far or near, I think to myself, "There is one of us well, at any rate,"—and with a sudden gush return to my senses.

Walt Whitman [1819–1892][10]

from Specimen Days

Abraham Lincoln

August 12th.—I see the President almost every day, as I happen to live where he passes to or from his lodgings out of town. He never sleeps at the White House during the hot season, but has quarters at a healthy location some three miles north of the city, the Soldiers' home, a United States military establishment. I saw him this morning about 8½ coming in to business, riding on Vermont avenue, near L street. He always has a company of twenty-five or thirty cavalry, with sabres drawn and held upright over their shoulders. They say this guard was against his personal wish, but he let his counselors have their way. The party makes no great show in uniform or horses. Mr. Lincoln on the saddle generally rides a good-sized, easy-going gray horse, is dress'd in plain black, somewhat rusty and dusty, wears a black stiff hat, and looks about as ordinary in attire, &c., as the commonest man. A lieutenant, with yellow straps, rides at his left, and following behind, two by two, come the cavalry men, in their yellow-striped jackets. They are generally going at a slow trot, as that is the pace set them by the one they wait upon. The sabres and accoutrements clank, and the entirely unornamental *cortège* as it trots toward Lafayette square arouses no sensation, only some curious stranger stops and gazes. I see very plainly Abraham Lincoln's dark brown face, with the deep-cut lines, the eyes, always to me with a deep latent sadness in the expression. We have got so that we exchange bows, and very cordial ones. Sometimes the President goes and comes in an open barouche. The cavalry always accompany him, with drawn sabres. Often I notice as he goes out evenings—and sometimes in the morning, when he returns early—he turns off and halts at the large and handsome residence of the Secretary of War, on K street, and holds conference there. If in his barouche, I can see from my window he does not alight, but sits in his vehicle, and Mr. Stanton comes out to attend him. Sometimes one of his sons, a boy of ten or twelve, accompanies him, riding at his right on a pony. Earlier in the summer I occasionally saw the President and his wife, toward the latter part of the afternoon, out in a barouche, on a pleasure ride through the city. Mrs. Lincoln was dress'd in complete black, with a long crape veil. The equipage is of the plainest kind, only two horses, and they nothing extra. They pass'd me once very close, and I saw the President in the face fully, as they were moving slowly, and his look, though abstracted, happen'd to be directed steadily in my eye. He bow'd and smiled, but far beneath his smile I noticed well the expression I have alluded to. None of the artists or pictures has caught the deep, though subtle and indirect expression of this man's face. There is something else there. One of the great portrait painters of two or three centuries ago is needed.

Death of a Wisconsin Officer

Another characteristic scene of that dark and bloody 1863, from notes of my visit to Armory-square hospital, one hot but pleasant summer day. In ward H we approach the cot of a young lieutenant of one of the Wisconsin regiments. Tread the bare board floor lightly here, for the pain and panting of death are in this cot. I saw the lieutenant when he was first brought here from Chancellorsville, and have been with him occasionally from day to day and night to night. He had been getting along pretty well till night before last, when a sudden hemorrhage that could not be stopt came upon him, and to-day it still continues at intervals. Notice that water-pail by the side of the bed, with a quantity of blood and bloody pieces of muslin, nearly full; that tells the story. The poor young man is struggling painfully for breath, his great dark eyes with a glaze already upon them, and the choking faint but audible in his throat. An attendant sits by him, and will not leave him till the last; yet little or nothing can be done. He will die here in an hour or two, without the presence of kith or kin. Meantime the ordinary chat and business of the ward a little way off goes on indifferently. Some of the inmates are laughing and joking, others are playing checkers or cards, others are reading, &c.

I have noticed through most of the hospitals that as long as there is any chance for a man, no matter how bad he may be, the surgeon and nurses work hard, sometimes with curious tenacity, for his life, doing everything, and keeping somebody by him to execute the doctor's orders, and minister to him every minute night and day. See that screen there. As you advance through the dusk of early candle-light, a nurse will step forth on tip-toe, and silently but imperiously forbid you to make any noise, or perhaps to come near at all. Some soldier's life is flickering there, suspended between recovery and death. Perhaps at this moment the exhausted frame has just fallen into a light sleep that a step might shake. You must retire. The neighboring patients must move in their stocking feet. I have been several times struck with such mark'd efforts—everything bent to save a life from the very grip of the destroyer. But when that grip is once firmly fix'd, leaving no hope or chance at all, the surgeon abandons the patient. If it is a case where stimulus is any relief, the nurse gives milk-punch or brandy, or whatever is wanted, *ad libitum.* There is no fuss made. Not a bit of sentimentalism or whining have I seen about a single death-bed in hospital or on the field, but generally impassive indifference. All is over, as far as any efforts can avail; it is useless to expend emotions or labors. While there is a prospect they strive hard—at least most surgeons do; but death certain and evident, they yield the field.

The Real War Will Never Get in the Books

And so good-bye to the war. I know not how it may have been, or may be, to others—to me the main interest I found, (and still, on recollection, find,) in the rank and file of the armies, both sides, and in those specimens amid the hospitals, and even the dead on the field. To me the points illustrating the latent personal character and eligibilities of these States, in the two or three millions of American young and middle-aged men, North and South, embodied in those armies—and especially the one-third or one-fourth of their number, stricken by wounds or disease at some time in the course of the contest—were of more significance even than the political interests involved. (As so much of a race depends on how it faces death, and how it stands personal anguish and sickness. As, in the glints of emotions under emergencies, and the indirect traits and asides in Plutarch, we get far profounder clues to the antique world than all its more formal history.)

Future years will never know the seething hell and the black infernal background of countless minor scenes and interiors, (not the official surface-courteousness of the Generals, not the few great battles) of the Secession war; and it is best they should not—the real war will never get in the books. In the mushy influences of current times, too, the fervid atmosphere and typical events of those years are in danger of being totally forgotten. I have at night watch'd by the side of a sick man in the hospital, one who could not live many hours. I have seen his eyes flash and burn as he raised himself and recurr'd to the cruelties on his surrender'd brother, and mutilations of the corpse afterward. (See, in the preceding pages, the incident at Upperville—the seventeen kill'd as in the description, were left there on the ground. After they dropt dead, no one touch'd them—all were made sure of, however. The carcasses were left for the citizens to bury or not, as they chose.)

Such was the war. It was not a quadrille in a ball-room. Its interior history will not only never be written—its practicality, minutiae of deeds and passions, will never be even suggested. The actual soldier of 1862-'65, North and South, with all his ways, his incredible dauntlessness, habits, practices, tastes, language, his fierce friendship, his appetite, rankness, his superb strength and animality, lawless gait, and a hundred unnamed lights and shades of camp, I say, will never be written—perhaps must not and should not be.

The preceding notes may furnish a few stray glimpses into that life, and into those lurid interiors, never to be fully convey'd to the future. The hospital part of the drama from '61 to '65, deserves indeed to be recorded. Of that many-threaded drama, with its sudden and strange surprises, its confounding of prophecies, its moments of despair, the dread of foreign interference, the interminable campaigns, the bloody battles, the mighty and cumbrous and green armies, the drafts and bounties—the immense money expenditure, like a heavy-pouring constant rain—with, over the whole land, the last three years of the struggle, an unending, universal mourning-wail of women, parents, orphans—the marrow of the tragedy concentrated in those Army Hospitals—(it seem'd sometimes as if the whole interest of the land, North and South, was one vast central hospital, and all the rest of the affair but flanges)—those forming the untold and unwritten history of the war—infinitely greater (like life's) than the few scraps and distortions that are ever told or written. Think how much, and of importance, will be—how much, civic and military, has already been—buried in the grave, in eternal darkness.

A July Afternoon by the Pond

The fervent heat, but so much more endurable in this pure air—the white and pink pond-blossoms, with great heart-shaped leaves; the glassy waters of the creek, the banks, with dense bushery, and the picturesque beeches and shade and turf; the tremulous, reedy call of some bird from recesses, breaking the warm, indolent, half-voluptuous silence; and occasional wasp, hornet, honey-bee or bumble (they hover near my hands or face, yet annoy me not, nor I them, as they appear to examine, find nothing, and away they go)—the vast space of the sky overhead so clear, and the buzzard up there sailing his slow whirl in majestic spirals and discs; just over the surface of the pond, two large slate-color'd dragon-flies, with wings of lace, circling and darting and occasionally balancing themselves quite still, their wings quivering all the time, (are they not showing off for my amusement?)—the pond itself, with the sword-shaped calamus; the water snakes—occasionally a flitting blackbird, with red dabs on his shoulders, as he darts slantingly by—the sounds that bring out the solitude, warmth, light and shade—the quawk of some pond duck—(the crickets and grasshoppers are mute in the noon heat, but I hear the song of the first cicadas;)—then at some distance the rattle and whirr of a reaping machine as the horses draw it on a rapid walk through a rye field on the opposite side of the creek—(what was the yellow or light-brown bird, large as a young hen, with short neck and long-stretch'd legs I just saw, in flapping and awkward flight over there through the trees?)—the prevailing delicate, yet palpable, spicy, grassy, clovery perfume to my nostrils; and over all, encircling all, to my sight and soul, the free space of the sky, transparent and blue—and hovering there in the west, a mass of white-gray fleecy clouds the sailors call "shoals of mackerel"—the sky, with silver swirls like locks of toss'd hair, spreading, expanding—a vast voiceless, formless simulacrum—yet may-be the most real reality and formulator of everything—who knows?

Loafing in the Woods

March 8.—I write this down in the country again, but in a new spot, seated on a log in the woods, warm, sunny, midday. Have been loafing here deep among the trees, shafts of tall pines, oak, hickory, with a thick undergrowth of laurels and grapevines—the ground cover'd everywhere by debris, dead leaves, breakage, moss—everything solitary, ancient, grim. Paths (such as they are) leading hither and yon—(how made I know not, for nobody seems to come here, nor man nor cattle-kind). Temperature to-day about 60, the wind through the pine-tops; I sit and listen to its hoarse sighing above (and to the *stillness*) long and long, varied by aimless rambles in the old roads and paths, and by exercise-pulls at the young saplings, to keep my joints from getting stiff. Blue-birds, robins, meadow-larks begin to appear.

Next day, 9th.—A snowstorm in the morning, and continuing most of the day. But I took a walk over two hours, the same woods and paths, amid the falling flakes. No wind, yet the musical low murmur through the pines, quite pronounced, curious, like waterfalls, now still'd, now pouring again. All the senses, sight, sound, smell, delicately gratified. Every snowflake lay where it fell on the evergreens, holly-trees, laurels, &c., the multitudinous leaves and branches piled, bulging-white, defined by edge-lines of emerald—the tall straight columns of the plentiful bronze-topt pines—a slight resinous odor blending with that of the snow. (For there is a scent to everything, even the snow, if you can only detect it—no two places, hardly any two hours, anywhere, exactly alike. How different the odor of noon from midnight, or winter from summer, or a windy spell from a still one.)

Jourdon Anderson [1825–1907][11]

Letter from a Freedman to His Old Master

Dayton, Ohio, August 7, 1865
To my old Master, Col. P. H. Henderson, Big Spring, Tennessee
Sir: I got your letter and was glad to find that you had not forgotten Jourdon, and that you wanted me to come back and live with you again, promising to do better for me than anybody else can. I have often felt uneasy about you. I thought the Yankees would have hung you long before this, for harboring Rebs they found at your house. I suppose they never heard about your going to Colonel Martin's to kill the Union soldier that was left by his company in their stable. Although you shot at me twice before I left you, I did not want to hear of your being hurt, and am glad you are still living. It would do me good to go back to the dear old home again, and see Miss Mary and Miss Martha and Allen, Esther, Green, and Lee. Give my love to them all, and tell them I hope we will meet in the better world, if not in this. I would have gone back to see you all when I was working in the Nashville Hospital, but one of the neighbors told me that Henry intended to shoot me if he ever got a chance.

I want to know particularly what the good chance is you propose to give me. I am doing tolerably well here. I get twenty-five dollars a month, with victuals and clothing; have a comfortable home for Mandy,—the folks call her Mrs. Anderson,—and the children—Milly, Jane, and Grundy—go to school and are learning well. The teacher says Grundy has a bead for a preacher. They go to Sunday school, and Mandy and me attend church regularly. We are kindly treated. Sometimes we overhear others saying, "Them colored people were slaves" down in Tennessee. The children feel hurt when they hear such remarks; but I tell them it was no disgrace in Tennessee to belong to Colonel Anderson. Many darkeys would have been proud, as I used to be, to call you master. Now if you will write and say what wages you will give me, I will be better able to decide whether it would be to my advantage to move back again.

As to my freedom, which you say I can have, there is nothing to be gained on that score, as I got my free papers in 1864 from the Provost-Marshal-General of the Department of Nashville. Mandy says she would be afraid to go back without some proof that you were disposed to treat us justly and kindly; and we have concluded to test your sincerity by asking you to send us our wages for the time we served you. This will make us forget and forgive old scores, and rely on your justice and friendship in the future. I served you faithfully for thirty-two years, and Mandy twenty years. At twenty-five dollars a month for me, and two dollars a week for Mandy, our earnings would amount to eleven thousand six hundred and eighty dollars. Add to this the interest for the time our wages have been kept back, and deduct what you paid for our clothing, and three doctor's visits to me, and pulling a tooth for Mandy, and the balance will show what we are in justice entitled to. Please send the money by Adams's Express, in care of V. Winters, Esq., Dayton, Ohio. If you fail to pay us for faithful labors in the past, we can have little faith in your promises in the future. We trust the good Maker has opened your eyes to the wrongs which you and your fathers have done to me and my fathers, in making us toil for you for generations without recompense. Here I draw my wages every Saturday night; but in Tennessee there was never any pay-day for the negroes any more than for the horses and cows. Surely there will be a day of reckoning for those who defraud the laborer of his hire.

In answering this letter, please state if there would be any safety for my Milly and Jane, who are now grown up, and both good-looking girls. You know how it was with poor Matilda and Catherine. I would rather stay here and starve—and die, if it come to that—than have my girls brought to shame by the violence and wickedness of their young masters. You will also please state if there has been any schools opened for the colored children in your neighborhood. The great desire of my life now is to give my children an education, and have them form virtuous habits.

Say howdy to George Carter, and thank him for taking the pistol from you when you were shooting at me.

From your old servant,

JOURDON ANDERSON

Dante Gabriel Rossetti [1828–1882][12]

The Cup of Water

The young King of a country is hunting on a day with a young Knight, his friend; when, feeling thirsty, he stops at a Forester's cottage, and the Forester's daughter brings him a cup of water to drink. Both of them are equally enamoured at once of her unequalled beauty. The King, however, has been affianced from boyhood to a Princess worthy of all love, and whom he has always believed he loved until undeceived by his new absorbing passion; but the Knight, resolved to sacrifice all other considerations to his love, goes again to the Forester's cottage and asks his daughter's hand. He finds that the girl has fixed her thoughts on the King, whose rank she does not know. On hearing it she tells her suitor humbly that she must die if such be her fate, but cannot love another. The Knight goes to the King to tell him all and beg his help; and the two friends then come to an explanation. Ultimately the King goes to the girl and pleads his friend's cause, not disguising his own passion, but saying that as he sacrifices himself to honor, so should she, at his prayer, accept a noble man whom he loves better than all men and whom she will love too. This she does at last; and the King makes his friend an Earl and gives him a grant of the forest and surrounding country as a marriage gift, with the annexed condition, that the Earl's wife shall bring the King a cup of water at the same spot on every anniversary of their first meeting when he rides a-hunting with her husband. At no other time will he see her, loving her too much. He weds the Princess, and thus two years pass, the condition being always fulfilled. But before the third anniversary the lady dies in childbirth, leaving a daughter. The King's life wears on, and still he and his friend pursue their practice of hunting on that day, for sixteen years. When the anniversary comes round for the sixteenth time since the lady's death, the Earl tells his daughter, who has grown to her mother's perfect likeness (but whom the King has never seen), to meet them on the old spot with the cup of water, as her mother first did when of the same age. The King, on seeing her, is deeply moved; but on her being presented to him by the Earl, he is about to take the cup from her hand, when he is aware of a second figure in her exact likeness but dressed in peasant's clothes, who steps to her side as he bends from his horse to take the cup, looks in his face with solemn words of love and welcome, and kisses him on the mouth. He falls forward on his horse's neck, and is lifted up dead.

Michael Scott's Wooing

Michael Scott and a friend, both young and dissolute, are returning from a carouse, by moonlight, along a wild sea-coast during a groundswell. As they come within view of a small house on the rocky shore, his companion taunts Michael Scott as to his known passion for the maiden Janet, who dwells there with her father, and as to the failure of the snares he has laid for her. Scott is goaded to great irritation, and as they near the point of the sands overlooked by the cottage, he turns round on his friend and declares that the maiden shall come out to him then and there at his summons. The friend still taunts and banters him, saying that wine has heated his brain; but Scott stands quite still, muttering, and regarding the cottage with a gesture of command. After he has done so for some time, the door opens softly, and Janet comes running down the rock. As she approaches, she nearly rushes into Michael Scott's arms, but instead swerves aside, runs swiftly by him, and plunges into the surging waves. With a shriek Michael plunges after her, and strikes out this side and that, and lashes his way among the billows, between the rising and sinking breakers; but all in vain, no sign appears of her. After some time spent in this way he returns almost exhausted to the sands, and passing without answer by his appalled and questioning friend, he climbs the rock to the door of the cottage, which is now closed. Janet's father answers his loud knocking, and to him he says, "Slay me, for your daughter has drowned herself this hour in yonder sea, and by my means." The father at first suspects some stratagem, but finally deems him mad, and says, "You rave,—my daughter is at rest in her bed." "Go seek her there," answers Michael Scott. The father goes up to his daughter's chamber, and returning very pale, signs to Michael to follow him. Together they climb the stair, and find Janet half lying and half kneeling, turned violently round, as if, in the act of rising from her bed, she had again thrown herself backward and clasped the feet of a crucifix at her bedhead; so she lies dead. Michael Scott rushes from the house, and returning maddened to the seashore, is with difficulty restrained from suicide by his friend. At last he stands like stone for a while, and then, as if repeating an inner whisper, he describes the maiden's last struggle with her heart. He says how she loved him but would not sin; how, hearing in her sleep his appeal from the shore, she almost yielded, and the embodied image of her longing came rushing out to him; but how in the last instant she turned back for refuge to Christ, and her soul was wrung from her by the struggle of her heart. "And as I speak," he says, "the fiend who whispers this concerning her says also in my ear how surely I am lost."

Mary Mapes Dodge [1831–1905][13]

Our Vegetables

In these days, when nearly all the good things in the vegetable world are fast becoming cosmopolitan, it is interesting to trace the nationality of some of the most familiar things in our daily fare. Seldom, while munching our matutinal radish, do we pause to conjure an imaginary bed of buried crimson and white in the far lands of Fang-Chou and Ptys-Wampi; yet from China and Japan were the first Radishes introduced to the outside barbarians of Europe. Neither, at supper, in meeting with a peculiarly flavorous morsel in our cake, do we inwardly thank the home of Demosthenes for the luxury; yet the earliest Citron-groves breathed their perfume on the sunny Grecian ether. Our Quinces, hanging from crooked, crowded limbs, the most neglected of all our luxuries, may be forced to stand in drunken rows along broken-down fences, or act as outposts to barns and outhouses; but the great-great-grand-mother of all the Quinces was a plucky little tree of high station, looked up to by sweet-scented shrubs in the Island of Crete.

Fennel grew wild along the banks of European rivers long before the first entertainment of the "Arabian Nights" was dreamed of; and Celery, once known as "Smallage," was munched by many an ancient Druid, let us believe, plucking it during his solitary walks along the old British coast. Even then, it may be, the ducks of an unknown continent were munching it too, for it grows wild upon our Chesapeake and Delaware bays, and our canvas-backs and their friends love to dine upon it. But the British, as usual, have all the credit, as it is down in their books.

Garlic came from Sicily, where, for my part, I wish it had stayed. The *Caulo-rapa*, an afflicted cross between the turnip and cabbage, claims the Vaterland for its own. Beans blossomed first within sight of embryo mummies, in the land of the Sphinx; and the Egg-plant first laid its glossy treasures under an African sun.

Peru and Chili were the first countries enlivened by the dazzling hues of the Nasturtian vine; and Southern Europe gave us the Artichoke and the Beet.

To Persia we stand indebted for Peaches, Walnuts, Mulberries, and a score of everyday luxuries and necessities; to Arabia we owe the cultivation of Spinage; and to Southern Europe we must bow in tearful gratitude for the Horse-radish.

At Siberia the victims of modern intemperance may shake their gory locks forever—for from that cold, unsocial land came Rye, the father of the great fire-water river which has floated so many jolly souls on its treacherous tides, and engulfed so much of humanity's treasure.

The Chestnut, dear to squirrels and young America, first dropped its burrs on Italian soil, while its giant cousin, yclept the "Horse," is a native of Thibet.

Who ever dreams, while enjoying his "Bergamotte," his "Flemish Beauty," or his "Jargonelle," that the first Pear-blossoms opened within sight of the Pyramids? and what fair school-girl of all the pickle-eating tribe, dreams of thanking the East Indies for her Cucumbers? Apropos of this, I once was told by a worthy old lady of Long Island, a singular item in regard to the last-named edible. She said that in its wild state it grew on very luxuriant vines that trailed in every direction over the ground, tangling themselves among the bushes at such a rate that the progress of grazing animals was thereby much impeded; hence, she assured me, the name, *cow-cumber.* The old lady's learning, I admit, was generally not of the most reliable order, but I give her suggestion for what it may be worth. Probably she was in some way akin to that other worthy old lady in New Jersey who, when asked by her city nephew, why in the world she called a certain vegetable "Sparrow-grass," replied, innocently:

"Well, child, I can't say where these names comes from gen'rally, but certain it's as plain as the nose on your face that sparrow-grass must get its name from the sparrows feedin' on it so plentiful when it's in seed."

The nephew chuckled inwardly, of course. But he, poor fellow, was ignorant in his turn; for *he* didn't know that Asparagus was first found in Russia and Poland; and that in its wild state, as gathered along the shores of Long Island Sound and elsewhere, it is a most delicious edible.

Parsley, that prettiest of all pretty greens, taking so naturally to our American soil that it seems quite to the manner born, is only a sojourner among us. Its native home is Sardinia, or, rather, there it first secured an acquaintanceship with civilized man. Onions, too, are only naturalized foreigners in America. I had hoped that in poetic justice research would prove this pathetic bulb to have sprung from the land of Niobe: but no; Egypt stretches forth her withered hand and claims the Onion as her own!

Maize and Potatoes, thank Heaven! can mock us with no foreign pedigree. They are ours—ours to command, to have, and to hold, from time's beginning to its ending, though England and Ireland bluster over "Corn" and "Praties" till they are hoarse. John Bull's corn-laws take in wide fields of waving grain of many names; but *our* Corn and Potatoes he can claim only as emigrants—American cousins, whose coming and vanishing can make the British lion caper or crouch at will.

Migratory Husbands

I never had one of them, thank heaven! but I know they must be dreadful—these heads of families who are forever popping up in new localities, with a "Lo! I'll build here. Here's a rising bit of property;" or, "This old cottage I'll renovate, clap on a wing and a piazza, live in it six months, and sell out at a bargain." Then those husbands who are forever shifting their business from place to place,—now to a village, now to a city, now to the backwoods,—a delightful time must their wives have of it! Never mind how faithful, devoted, and enterprising a woman may be, it's a great trial for her to be continually pulling up stakes, and tearing away home-tendrils, even if her migratory spouse is in other respects the best in the world. I'd like to see the person who would tell me that I wouldn't go with John, if he decided to set up a soda-fountain in the Desert of Sahara. No. I'd go; but I should suffer in the going, though I told my woes not even to old Cheops himself. But what if, instead of one grand move, he flitted about like a grasshopper? What if he tried Bloomfield, and Flatbush, and Woodside, and Harlem, and a dozen other places, from the coming of the first nursery-tooth to the going away of the last nursery-measles? What if he dipped the children into twenty schools, filled every April air with mournful farewells to all our neighbors, and kept the parlor carpets in a perpetual spasm of contraction and expansion? Could I be the blessed, happy woman that I am? Shouldn't I be thin, weary, and heart-sore, and the children morally just little waifs made of the shreds and patches of many villages? Certainly. Far be it from me to question established similes of wifehood: but your oaks don't hop about. They stand still and give the clinging vines a chance to take root beside them.

Only yesterday, while shopping in town, I chanced to find myself in a street-car beside a man and a stout woman engaged in earnest conversation. His was a thin, flushed face, with restless eyes, and lips that asked "Why?" "Who?" "Where?" even when they were silent. Hers was soft, fleshy, massive;

and its little eyes were full of temporary affability and interest. He evidently was speaking of some recent bereavement, while the lady leaning toward him wore a sort of wash of deep feeling which was "not a dye," though it gave her a hue of sympathy quite proper in a street-car. Presently I caught the words,—

"She was in-deed. You lost a treasure when you lost *her.*"

"Yes, and a wonderful creature for moving about," pursued the man, with deep feeling. "It didn't make any difference: you could take that woman, and *set her down anywhere!*"

His eyes filled with tears; and I looked out of the window, sorry for his sake, but glad that the angels had taken at least one poor woman away from a migratory husband.

The country abounds with these naturalized Bedouins. I say nothing against men who go North, South, East, or West, and settle. They are the nerves of the body politic, and indispensable to our new civilization. But I do feel impelled to quote mother's favorite expression, and whisper to hundreds of men within hearing distance at this moment, "Do stay put." For the sake of wives, home, children, yourselves, take root somewhere. Help to build up in America the beautiful homestead feeling common to Europeans, and almost unknown to us. Let your very saplings understand that in time they are to shade your great-great-grand-children.

Ada Clare [Jane McElhenney, 1834–1874][14]

The Slave of the House

Any persons suppose the Inquisition to have ceased to exist. They are an ill-advised body. That organized system of torment, in its concentrated and virulent type, has ceased to exist; but the spirit of the thing, in a mild but universal form, thrives ever in the shape of the first class brown stone and basement house, high stoop, with all the modern improvements.

I know a young man, now a resident of Bedlam, who was driven into that kingdom by the cruel treatment of a House. He had been for some years in Paris, where he had learned all manner of pleasant, cheerful, and natural habits. On returning to this city, he took up his abode in the residence of his sister-in-law, under the ensnaring promise that he should find there every comfort of home, in the bosom of his family.

Alas, me! How soon he found that the House was a merciless Juggernaut, before which he was obliged to throw himself down each day, and be crushed by its thousand-wheeled system of inexorable rules.

Fillipo, that was the victim's name, worshipped the Sun as a great sanitary monarch, and so, in the matter of getting up, followed that monarch—at a very respectful distance. But the impious House defied the solar sovereign, and gave forth its relentless fiat—breakfast at seven in winter. So while the earth was still wrapped in its ghastly blue mantle of daylight, while a thousand reeking dews and exhalations breathed out poison to the air, Fillipo crawled shivering from his bed, and thence down to a breakfast far which he had no appetite at that demoniac hour.

After this cheerful meal, Fillipo fain would have smoked a cigar, for, as his business did not claim him until twelve, there was at least four hours to be disposed of. Here, again, the House set its elephant's foot on his neck. Smoking anywhere in the body of the House, could only be equaled in its effects by a juvenile earthquake. The House, with its delicate nerves, would, in a fit of sneezing, have burst its cerements, and then ——. It was not necessary to urge this upon him, for he meekly felt that tobacco out of his own room was impossible.

His room did not seem exactly built with a convivial view. It was on the fourth story, a North room, without a fireplace, and the thermometer standing two degrees below zero. However, by means of putting on two overcoats and a shawl, by borrowing the blankets and counterpane from the bed to envelop his legs, and with his aunt's flannel petticoat and her muff on his head, he was enabled to have a pretty comfortable time, considering——considering Sir John Franklin.

Little by little the dreadful tyranny of the House was unfolded to his mind. Dinner was just at the most uncomfortable hour. At eleven o'clock at night the doors of this prison were barred and bolted. Fillipo was passionately fond of the theatre, but he must either sneak away ere the crisis of the play was worked out, or risk the ringing of the bell of his domicile, in which latter case he was kept out in the snow, an hour or so for private meditation, and then obliged to face an enraged and dangerous housemaid.

Poor Fillipo! Sunday was the toppling point of his anguish. He was of an extremely domestic turn, and loved to spend that day at home in an atmosphere of pipes and newspapers. But first of all, the piety, the morality, the social standing of the House demanded that the neighbors, who were supposed to be keenly watching its deportment, should see him go to church at least once each Sunday. And he went.

Newspapers were not allowed in the parlors, they were said to make a litter. Fillipo, who loved children, and was particularly attached to the baby, begged that he might occasionally bring her into the parlor, but, of course, his request was denied. There was no telling what mischief her little fingers might do. Fillipo felt that the baby was the only human being in the establishment. All the rest of them marched their life through in a funeral procession, before the muffled drum of the House.

One Sunday, while sitting in the best parlor, it occurred to Fillipo that while that room was extremely desolate, a warm sea of rich sunlight was rippling its glory against the closed and curtained windows. Acting on this suggestion he threw open the windows, and in tumbled a whole torrent of sun-splendor, to inundate with its bright waves, the grim majesty of the room. Hardly was this accomplished, when the entrance and remonstrance of his sister taught him that even the sunshine of heaven must not visit the House's cheek too roughly. Besides, the sun might fade its curtains. He gave a patient look around the room, and finding that all the furniture in it was equally under the iron rule, be bowed his head like a lamb and submitted. He saw that the House's chairs and sofas, though of a rich material, could not be seen, they were covered up with a cold and hideous linen cloth. That its mirrors, gas-fixtures, etc., though of the extremest elegance, could not be seen either, for the impenetrable, saffron-hued tarleton that enveloped them.

He sat down in a straight-backed chair—he had been warned against using the cushioned ones—and leaned his head back in dejection. Then and there his sister took occasion to tell him that his manner of sitting in her chairs was extremely painful to her. Leaning on the backs of the chairs rubbed off their gilding, dropping his hands tarnished their sides, and his habit of resting this heels firmly on the carpet gave a depression to the velvety nap of the same.

He meekly obeyed her, as she spoke, sitting with his toes slightly touching the ground, his hands in a distorted clasp on his knees, and his spine bullied into self-support, rigidly and awfully upright.

From that moment Reason began to totter on its throne. He wandered about the House a mild and harmless idiot, the sport of the housemaids, the compassion of the children, the contempt of the heads of the family. His habits, his heart, his spirits were all broken.

Oh, gentle youth! thou were not strong enough to bear the torture of custom. Regularity and punctiliousness have murdered thy peace. No more shalt thou whistle at the office, weep with enthusiasm at the opera, nor shall thy name ever more be set over sweet verses in the *Weekly Honeysuckle!*

Oh, gentlest of hearts, sweetest of tenor voices, most gallant of beaux! where art thou now?—treading the halls of Bloomingdale. Waiting for the time when thou shalt find rest in that Mansion, whose floors are paved with gold, that the world's idol and king may be trodden under foot, where the soul triumphs over fashion, where the perfectness of life blots out the rasping demands of rule and convention, and the only roof and walls is the pure, grand blue heaven of the gods.

Celia Thaxter [1835–1894][15]

from An Island Garden

[May] 15th. A thick fog wrapped the world in dimness early this morning; at eight o'clock it was rolling off and piling itself in glorious headlands over the coast, gleaming snow-white in the sun, but here and there thin silver strips lay across distant sails and islands, lingering as if loath to leave the earth for the sky. I took the baskets of plants I had found necessary to dig up to give the rest room, and paddled across to the next island in a little lapstreaked dory, to give them to my neighbors for their flower plots. Great is the pleasure in the giving and the taking. It was such a heavenly morning, so blue and calm after the tumult of yesterday! Along the far-off coast the joyous hills seemed laughing in the sunshine, and the great sea rippled all over with smiles.

From the low shores of the islands came the singing of the birds over the still water, with an indescribably quiet and peaceful effect, and as I rowed into the cove of my destination, passing the coasts of the little island called Malaga, I saw outlined against the sky the lovely grasses already blossoming among the rocks. A kingbird sat on a boulder and meditated; there was no tree, so he was fain to be content with a rock to sit on. I passed him almost near enough to touch him with my oar, but he did not stir, not he! My errand done and the plants distributed, I hastened back to my own dear little plot again, and up and down all the paths I went, digging out every unwelcome root of grass, plantain, mallow, catnip, clover, and the rest, once more raking them clear and clean. Outside, in a bed by itself, I sunk four pots of repotted Chrysanthemums, to be ready for the windows in early winter. All along the piazza are the house plants waiting to be attended to, cut back, repotted, and the soil enriched for winter blooming. Every day I attend to them, a few at a time. I cannot spare much time from my planting, weeding, watering, transplanting, and so forth, in the garden, but soon they will be all done. Began to transplant a few of the hundreds of the main body of Sweet Pea plants into the ground, carefully covering each bed as I finished with breadths of light mosquito netting to make them sparrow-proof. As I was working busily I heard the sweet calling of curlews, and looking up saw six of them wheeling overhead. Such sociable birds! They replied to my challenge as if I had been one of themselves, and as long as their calls were answered, lingered near, but being forgotten presently drifted off on the wind, their clear whistle sounding fainter and fainter as they were lost in the distance. All the rest of this day was spent in setting out Sweet Peas, and it will take more than a whole day more to finish, for I put them all round against the fence outside, and into every space I can spare for them within. After tea I hunted slugs as usual, and scattered ashes and lime, but I really feel that my friends the toads have done me the inestimable favor of reducing their hideous numbers, for certainly there are less than last year so far. Early in April, as I was vigorously hoeing in a corner, I unearthed a huge toad, to my perfect delight and satisfaction; he had lived all winter, he had doubtless fed on slugs all the autumn. I could have kissed him on the spots. Very carefully I placed him in the middle of a large green clump of tender Columbine. He really wasn't more than half awake, after his long winter nap, but he was alive and well, and when later I went to look after him, lo! he had crept off, perhaps to snuggle into the earth once more for another nap, till the sun should have a little more power.

To our great joy the frogs that we imported last year are also alive. We heard the soft rippling of their voices with the utmost pleasure; it is a lovely liquid-sweet sound. They have not lived over a winter here before. We feared that the vicinity of so much salt water might be injurious to them, but this year they have survived, and perhaps they may be established for good.

May 20th. All the past days have been filled with transplanting and the most vigorous weeding. In these five days the Sweet Peas have grown so tall I was obliged to go after sticks for them to-day, wheeling my light wheelbarrow up over the hill and across the island toward the south, where among the old ruined walls of cellars and houses, and little, almost erased garden plots, the thick growth of Bayberry and Elder offered me all the sticks I needed. Such a charming business was this! So beautiful the narrow road all the way, bordered by the lovely Shad-bush in bridal white, the delicate red Cherry with flowers so like Hawthorn as to be frequently mistaken for it, the pink Chokecherry, the common Wild Cherry (which seems to attract to itself most of the caterpillars in the land), all blossoming for dear life, and among thickets of Blackberry, Raspberry, Gooseberry, Wild Currant, Winterberry, Spirea, and I know not what, such crowds of flowers! The last of the gay golden Erythroniums, the Dogtooth Violets, dancing in the breeze; the large, softly-colored Anemones, now nearing their end; the banks of pearly Eyebrights; the white

Violets, lowly and fragrant; the straw-colored Uvularia; the ivory spikes of Solomon's Seal, just breaking into bloom, with its companion, the starry Trientalis; the tufts of Fern in cool clefts of rocks—of these I gathered several clumps for my fernery in the shade of the piazza. It would take too long to tell of all the flowers I saw, but one more I must mention. At the upper edge of a little cove at the southwest, where the old settlement of more than a hundred years ago was thickest, the earth was blue with the pretty Gill-go-over-the-ground, its charming blossoms covering the green turf and cropping out among the loose stones,—a dear, quaint little flower in two shades of blue marked with rich red-purple. It was too early for the Pimpernel to be in bloom, but the pink Herb Robert was out, the smallest of all the Geranium family, and I saw ranks of Goldenrod more than a foot high getting ready for autumn. To tell all I saw and all I loved and rejoiced in would take a whole day. Oh, the green and brown and golden mosses, the lovely, lowly growths along the way, and oh, the birds that sang and the waves that leaped and murmured along the shore! The sweet sky and the soft clouds, the far sails, the full joy of the summer morning, who shall tell it? I was so happy trundling home my barrow load of sticks piled to toppling, and finally tipping it up at the garden gate. It took the whole afternoon to stick the Peas, and I enjoyed every moment of it. Before putting the dry brittle branches in the ground, with a small, light hoe I went all over and through the earth about the Sweet Peas, uprooting chickweed and clover, pigweed and dogfennel, till there was not a weed to be seen near them. When night fell I had only just finished this pleasant work.

Elizabeth Stuart Phelps [1844–1911][16]

How Shall Women Dress?

The corset, even when not unreasonably worn or "laced," compresses the dimensions of the waist eight inches from their normal measurement. This has been repeatedly proved.

I have been told by the leading teacher of elocution in this country that he was forced to abandon the use of certain calisthenic exercises important to his art, because he found that the dress of the pupils forbade them to lift their arms above their heads.

"The very women who want their skirts trimmed most heavily," said a fashionable dress-maker, "are the ones whose backs ache so that they cannot stand long enough for me to try on their dresses."

"Every one of those spots," frankly said a distinguished oculist, pointing to a dotted lace veil, "every one of those spots is worth five dollars to me."

"My ladies," testifies another *modiste*, "are coming to me and saying, 'Make me look like Circe Cleopatra.' (Naming a beautiful and famous and favorite actress.) I answer, 'Madame, would you have of me the impossible? Circe Cleopatra has never worn a corset. That grace, that suppleness, that charm, that ease with which you observe how the lines of her costume follow the contour of her figure—Madame, no dress-make on God's earth can create you those things out of a French corset!' "

"My patrons," writes the manager of one of the oldest and largest enterprises for the sale of what is called the reformed underclothing, "are now chiefly fashionable women. Ten years ago, when we began struggling against the current, I had only strong-minded women. To-day, they are in the minority. My customers are society ladies ten to one."

Facts are arguments. These few representative ones are contributed to this discussion without the interference of comment.

Mary P. Thacher [1844–1941][17]

Passenger Pigeons

For many days the fresh morning air had resounded with the dull bumming of the prairie-chickens, and an unbroken line of snowy "schooners," as the emigrant-wagons are called on the prairies, had slowly moved westward. These wagons were followed by droves of cattle; and the cattle were driven by brown, dusty women, barefooted, and scantily clothed in blue drilling or patched and faded chintz. I had looked curiously at the labor-saving churns in which butter was made by the mere motion of the jolting wagons; I had questioned the rough-looking Germans and Norwegians, who often could not speak a word of English; and I was never weary of watching for the bright eyes of the dingy-faced little children, who sometimes peeped from the wagons. When these weary travelers halted by the wayside, and their gypsy fires blazed out into the night, what wild sweet singing was borne across the prairie on the evening breeze!

But one day I forgot my slow-plodding friends, in the excitement of watching the passage of a multitude of travelers who could no more be numbered than the sands upon the sea-shore. What a commotion the shy strangers made that early May morning! I was startled from sleep by a voice crying, "The pigeons!" and a strange sound, like the rushing of a strong wind, came to my ears. The air was full of flying birds, and for hours I watched the immense flock pass over that little prairie village in Minnesota. The birds flew very low, and hundreds of them alighted on the trees in passing. They often alight in such numbers that great branches are broken off, and sometimes the pigeons are crushed to death. The fields bordering the river were covered with them; but they only stopped to rest, apparently, or perhaps to pick up a little food, and were again on the wing. As these detachments of the vast army of pigeons rose from the ground, with a great flapping of wings, others alighted; meanwhile the main flock was passing steadily over our heads. The procession seemed endless, for the day wore on, and still the swift-winged birds rustled through the air, and still the coming flocks looked like delicate pencilings on the distant sky. It was a rare day for sportsmen. Instead of roosting in a neighboring forest, as we had hoped, the pigeons flew over into Wisconsin. But every day through the summer stray flocks foraged among the oak groves about us, and their shadows swept over sunny slopes and fields of waving grain, like flitting clouds.

From their nesting-place the birds flew all over Minnesota, Iowa, and Wisconsin in quest of food; but they always returned as the sun went down, though the roost was hundreds of miles distant. Audubon says that these pigeons travel at the rate of a mile in a minute, and that if one of them were to follow the fashion, and take a trip to Europe, it could cross the ocean in less than three days. When they fly through the woods, the sound of their wings is almost deafening; an old farmer compares it to the roar of ten thousand threshing-machines! But quite as wonderful as their speed is the great power of vision these birds possess. As they journey through space, they can overlook hundreds of acres at once, and their sharp eyes can discover at a glance whether the country beneath them is barren, or supplied with the food they need. The piece of woods that the pigeons selected in which to rear their young is three or four miles wide and ten miles long. Their nests were in every tree; sometimes more than fifty nests could be seen in one tree. In each of these frail nests, carelessly woven of a few twigs, two white shining eggs were laid.

When the young pigeons or squabs are almost ready to fly, comes the exciting time known as robbing the roost. Men arm themselves with long poles, with which they upset the nests; the poor squabs fall to the ground, and are easily caught in large numbers. They can then be kept in cages, fattened, and killed as they are wanted.

The passenger pigeon does not migrate from one part of the country to another to find a warmer climate, but only in search of food. So many of these birds are killed every year, for the New York and other markets, that it seems as if they must gradually disappear. But they multiply very rapidly, and Audubon thought that nothing but the destruction of our forests could lessen their number.

Emma Lazarus [1849–1887][18]

By the Waters of Babylon: Little Poems in Prose

I. The Exodus (August 3, 1492)

1. The Spanish noon is a blaze of azure fire, and the dusty pilgrims crawl like an endless serpent along treeless plains and bleached high-roads, through rock-split ravines and castellated, cathedral-shadowed towns.

2. The hoary patriarch, wrinkled as an almond shell, bows painfully upon his staff. The beautiful young mother, ivory-pale, well-nigh swoons beneath her burden; in her large enfolding arms nestles her sleeping babe, round her knees flock her little ones with bruised and bleeding feet. "Mother, shall we soon be there?"

3. The youth with Christ-like countenance speaks comfortably to father and brother, to maiden and wife. In his breast, his own heart is broken.

4. The halt, the blind, are amid the train. Sturdy pack-horses laboriously drag the tented wagons wherein lie the sick athirst with fever.

5. The panting mules are urged forward with spur and goad; stuffed are the heavy saddle-bags with the wreckage of ruined homes.

6. Hark to the tinkling silver hells that adorn the tenderly-carried silken scrolls,

7. In the fierce noon glare a lad bears a kindled lamp; behind its network of bronze the airs of heaven breathe not upon its faint purple star.

8. Noble and abject, learned and simple, illustrious and obscure, plod side by side, all brothers now, all merged in one routed army of misfortune.

9. Woe to the straggler who falls by the wayside! no friend shall close his eyes.

10. They leave behind, the grape, the olive, and the fig; the vines they planted, the corn they sowed, the garden-cities of Andalusia and Aragon, Estremadura and La Mancha, of Granada and Castile; the altar, the hearth, and the grave of their fathers.

11. The townsman spits at their garments, the shepherd quits his flock, the peasant his plow, to pelt with curses and stones; the villager sets on their trail his yelping cur.

12. Oh the weary march, oh the uptorn roots of home, oh the blankness

of the receding goal!

13. Listen to their lamentation: *They that ate dainty food are desolate in the streets; they that were reared in scarlet embrace dunghills. They flee away and wander about. Men say among the nations, they shall no more sojourn there; our end is near, our days are full, our doom is come.*

14. Whither shall they turn? for the West hath cast them out, and the East refuseth to receive.

15. O bird of the air, whisper to the despairing exiles, that to-day, to-day, from the many-masted, gayly-bannercd port of Palos, sails the world-unveiling Genoese, to unlock the golden gates of sunset and bequeath a Continent to Freedom!

II. Treasures

1. Through cycles of darkness the diamond sleeps in its coal-black prison.

2. Purely incrusted in its scaly casket, the breath-tarnished pear slumbers in mud and ooze.

3. Buried in tile bowels of earth, rugged and obscure, lies the ingot of gold.

4. Long hast thou been buried, O Israel, in the bowels of earth; long hast thou slumbered beneath the overwhelming waves; long hast thou slept in the rayless house of darkness.

5. Rejoice and sing, for only thus couldst thou rightly guard the golden knowledge, Truth, the delicate pearl and the adamantine jewel of the Law.

III. The Sower

1. Over a boundless plain went a man, carrying seed.

2. His face was blackened by sun and rugged from tempest, scarred and distorted by pain. Naked to the loins, his back was ridged with furrows, his breast was plowed with stripes.

3. From his hand dropped the fecund seed.

4. And behold, instantly started from the prepared soil a blade, a sheaf, a springing trunk, a myriad-branching, cloud-aspiring tree. Its arms touched the ends of the horizon, the heavens were darkened with its shadow.

5. It bare blossoms of gold and blossoms of blood, fruitage of health and fruitage of poison; birds sang amid its foliage, and a serpent was coiled about its stem.

6. Under its branches a divinely beautiful man, crowned with thorns, was nailed to a cross.

7. And the tree put forth treacherous boughs to strangle the Sower; his flesh was bruised and torn, but cunningly he disentangled the murderous knot and passed to the eastward.

8. Again there dropped from his band the fecund seed.

9. And behold, instantly started from the prepared soil a blade, a sheaf, a springing trunk, a myriad-branching, cloud-aspiring tree. Crescent-shaped like little emerald moons were the leaves; it bare blossoms of silver and blossoms of blood, fruitage of health and fruitage of poison; birds sang amid its foliage and a serpent was coiled about its stem.

10. Under its branches a turbaned mighty-limbed Prophet brandished a drawn sword.

11. And behold, this tree likewise puts forth perfidious arms to strangle the Sower; but cunningly he disentangles the murderous knot and passes on.

12. Lo, his hands are not empty of grain, the strength of his arm is not spent.

13. What germ hast thou saved for the future, O miraculous Husbandman? Tell me, thou Planter of Christhood and Islam; tell me, thou seed-bearing Israel!

IV. The Test

1. Daylong I brooded upon the Passion of Israel.

2. I saw him bound to the wheel, nailed to the cross, cut off by the sword, burned at the stake, tossed into the seas.

3. And always the patient, resolute, martyr face arose in silent rebuke and defiance.

4. A Prophet with four eyes; wide gazed the orbs of the spirit above the sleeping eyelids of the senses.

5. A Poet, who plucked from his bosom the quivering heart and fashioned it into a lyre.

6. A placid-browed Sage, uplifted from earth in celestial meditation.

7. These I saw, with princes and people in their train; the monumental dead and the standard-bearers of the future.

8. And suddenly I heard a burst of mocking laughter, and turning, I beheld the shuffling gait, the ignominious features, the sordid mask of the son of the Ghetto.

V. Currents

1. Vast oceanic movements, the flux and reflux of immeasurable tides oversweep our continent.

2. From the far Caucasian steppes, from the squalid Ghettos of Europe,

3. From Odessa and Bucharest, from Kief and Ekaterinoslav,

4. Hark to the cry of the exiles of Babylon, the voice of Rachel mourning for her children, of Israel lamenting for Zion.

5. And lo, like a turbid stream, the long-pent flood bursts the dykes of oppression and rushes hitherward.

6. Unto her ample breast, the generous mother of nations welcomes them.

7. The herdsman of Canaan and the seed of Jerusalem's royal shepherd renew their youth amid the pastoral plains of Texas and the golden valleys of the Sierras.

VI. The Prophet

1. Moses ben Maimon lifting his perpetual lamp over the path of the perplexed;

2. Hallevi, the honey-tongued poet, wakening amid the silent ruins of Zion the sleeping lyre of David;

3. Moses, the wise son of Mendel, who made the Ghetto illustrious;

4. Abarbanel, the counselor of kings; Alcharisi, the exquisite singer; Ibn Ezra, the perfect old man; Gabirol, the tragic seer;

5. Heine, the enchanted magician, the heart-broken jester;

6. Yea, and the century-crowned patriarch whose bounty engirdles the globe;—

7. These need no wreath and no trumpet; like perennial asphodel blossoms, their fame, their glory resounds like the brazen-throated comet.

8. But thou—hast thou faith in the fortune of Israel? Wouldst thou lighten the anguish of Jacob?

9. Then shalt thou take the hand of yonder caftaned wretch with flowing curls and gold-pierced ears;

10. Who crawls blinking forth from the loathsome recesses of the Jewry;

11. Nerveless his fingers, puny his frame; haunted by the bat-like phantoms of superstition is his brain.

12. Thou shalt say to the bigot, "My Brother," and to the creature of darkness, "My Friend."

13. And thy heart shall spend itself in fountains of love upon the ignorant, the coarse, and the abject.

14. Then in the obscurity thou shalt hear a rush of wings, thine eyes shall be bitten with pungent smoke.

15. And close against thy quivering lips shall be pressed the live coal wherewith the Seraphim brand the Prophets,

VII. Chrysalis

1. Long, long has the Orient-Jew spun around his helplessness the cunningly enmeshed web of Talmud and Kabbala.

2. Imprisoned in dark corners of misery and oppression, closely he drew about him the dust-gray filaments, soft as silk and stubborn as steel, until he lay death-stiffened in mummied seclusion.

3. And the world has named him an ugly worm, shunning the blessed daylight.

4. But when the emancipating springtide breathes wholesome, quickening airs, when the Sun of Love shines out with cordial fires, lo, the Soul of Israel bursts her cobweb sheath, and flies forth attired in the winged beauty of immortality.

Kate Chopin [1850–1904][19]

Ripe Figs

Maman-Nainaine said that when the figs were ripe Babette might go to visit her cousins down on the Bayou-Lafourche where the sugar cane grows. Not that the ripening of figs had the least thing to do with it, but that is the way Maman-Nainaine was.

It seemed to Babette a very long time to wait; for the leaves upon the trees were tender yet, and the figs were like little hard, green marbles.

But warm rains came along and plenty of strong sunshine, and though Maman-Nainaine was as patient as the statue of la Madone, and Babette as restless as a humming-bird, the first thing they both knew it was hot summer-time. Every day Babette danced out to where the fig-trees were in a long line against the fence. She walked slowly beneath them, carefully peering between the gnarled, spreading branches. But each time she came disconsolate away again. What she saw there finally was something that made her sing and dance the whole long day.

When Maman-Nainaine sat down in her stately way to breakfast, the following morning, her muslin cap standing like an aureole about her white, placid face, Babette approached. She bore a dainty porcelain platter, which she set down before her godmother. It contained a dozen purple figs, fringed around with their rich, green leaves.

"Ah," said Maman-Nainaine, arching her eyebrows, "how early the figs have ripened this year!"

"Oh," said Babette, "I think they have ripened very late."

"Babette," continued Maman-Nainaine, as she peeled the very plumpest figs with her pointed silver fruit-knife, "you will carry my love to them all down on Bayou-Lafourche. And tell your Tante Frosine I shall look for her at Toussaint—when the chrysanthemums are in bloom."

An Idle Fellow

I am tired. At the end of these years I am very tired. I have been studying in books the languages of the living and those we call dead. Early in the fresh morning I have studied in books, and throughout the day when the sun was shining; and at night when there were stars, I have lighted my oil-lamp and studied in books. Now my brain is weary and I want rest.

I shall sit here on the door-step beside my friend Paul. He is an idle fellow with folded hands. He laughs when I upbraid him, and bids me, with a motion, hold my peace. He is listening to a thrush's song that comes from the blur of yonder apple-tree. He tells me the thrush is singing a complaint. She wants her mate that was with her last blossom-time and builded a nest with her. She will have no other mate. She will call for him till she hears the notes of her beloved-one's song coming swiftly towards her across forest and field.

Paul is a strange fellow. He gazes idly at a billowy white cloud that rolls lazily over and over along the edge of the blue sky.

He turns away from me and the words with which I would instruct him, to drink deep the scent of the clover-field and the thick perfume from the rose-hedge.

We rise from the door-step and walk together down the gentle slope of the hill; past the apple-tree, and the rose-hedge; and along the border of the field where wheat is growing. We walk down to the foot of the gentle slope where women and men and children are living.

Paul is a strange fellow. He looks into the faces of people who pass us by. He tells me that in their eyes he reads the story of their souls. He knows men and women and the little children, and why they look this way and that way. He knows the reasons that turn them to and fro and cause them to go and come. I think I shall walk a space through the world with my friend Paul. He is very wise, he knows the language of God which I have not learned.

The Story of an Hour

Knowing that Mrs. Mallard was afflicted with a heart trouble, great care was taken to break to her as gently as possible the news of her husband's death.

It was her sister Josephine who told her, in broken sentences; veiled hints that revealed in half concealing. Her husband's friend Richards was there, too, near her. It was he who had been in the newspaper office when intelligence of the railroad disaster was received, with Brently Mallard's name leading the list of "killed." He had only taken the time to assure himself of its truth by a second telegram, and had hastened to forestall any less careful, less tender friend in bearing the sad message.

She did not hear the story as many women have heard the same, with a paralyzed inability to accept its significance. She wept at once, with sudden, wild abandonment, in her sister's arms. When the storm of grief had spent itself she went away to her room alone. She would have no one follow her.

There stood, facing the open window, a comfortable, roomy armchair. Into this she sank, pressed down by a physical exhaustion that haunted her body and seemed to reach into her soul.

She could see in the open square before her house the tops of trees that were all aquiver with the new spring life. The delicious breath of rain was in the air. In the street below a peddler was crying his wares. The notes of a distant song which some one was singing reached her faintly, and countless sparrows were twittering in the eaves.

There were patches of blue sky showing here and there through the clouds that had met and piled one above the other in the west facing her window.

She sat with her head thrown back upon the cushion of the chair, quite motionless, except when a sob came up into her throat and shook her, as a child who has cried itself to sleep continues to sob in its dreams.

She was young, with a fair, calm face, whose lines bespoke repression and even a certain strength. But now there was a dull stare in her eyes, whose gaze was fixed away off yonder on one of those patches of blue sky. It was not a glance of reflection, but rather indicated a suspension of intelligent thought.

There was something coming to her and she was waiting for it, fearfully. What was it? She did not know; it was too subtle and elusive to name. But she felt it, creeping out of the sky, reaching toward her through the sounds, the scents, the color that filled the air.

Now her bosom rose and fell tumultuously. She was beginning to recognize this thing that was approaching to possess her, and she was striving to beat it back with her will—as powerless as her two white slender hands would have been.

When she abandoned herself a little whispered word escaped her slightly parted lips. She said it over and over under her breath: "free, free, free!" The vacant stare and the look of terror that had followed it went from her eyes. They stayed keen and bright. Her pulses beat fast, and the coursing blood warmed and relaxed every inch of her body.

She did not stop to ask if it were or were not a monstrous joy that held her. A clear and exalted perception enabled her to dismiss the suggestion as trivial.

She knew that she would weep again when she saw the kind, tender hands folded in death; the face that had never looked save with love upon her, fixed and gray and dead. But she saw beyond that bitter moment a long procession of years to come that would belong to her absolutely. And she opened and spread her arms out to them in welcome.

There would be no one to live for her during those coming years; she would live for herself. There would be no powerful will bending hers in that blind persistence with which men and women believe they have a right to impose a private will upon a fellow-creature. A kind intention or a cruel intention made the act seem no less a crime as she looked upon it in that brief moment of illumination.

And yet she had loved him—sometimes. Often she had not. What did it matter! What could love, the unsolved mystery, count for in face of this possession of self-assertion which she suddenly recognized as the strongest impulse of her being!

"Free! Body and soul free!" she kept whispering.

Josephine was kneeling before the closed door with her lips to the keyhole, imploring for admission. "Louise, open the door! I beg; open the door—you will make yourself ill. What are you doing, Louise? For heaven's sake open the door."

"Go away. I am not making myself ill." No; she was drinking in a very elixir of life through that open window.

Her fancy was running riot along those days ahead of her. Spring days, and summer days, and all sorts of days that would be her own. She breathed a quick prayer that life might be long. It was only yesterday she had thought with a shudder that life might be long.

She arose at length and opened the door to her sister's importunities. There was a feverish triumph in her eyes, and she carried herself unwittingly like a goddess of Victory. She clasped her sister's waist, and together they descended the stairs. Richards stood waiting for them at the bottom.

Some one was opening the front door with a latchkey. It was Brently Mallard who entered, a little travel-stained, composedly carrying his grip-sack and umbrella. He had been far from the scene of accident, and did not even know there had been one. He stood amazed at Josephine's piercing cry; at

Richards' quick motion to screen him from the view of his wife.

But Richards was too late.

When the doctors came they said she had died of heart disease—of joy that kills.

The Night Came Slowly

I am losing my interest in human beings; in the significance of their lives and their actions. Some one has said it is better to study one man than ten books. I want neither books nor men; they make me suffer. Can one of them talk to me like the night—the Summer night? Like the stars or the caressing wind?

The night came slowly, softly, as I lay out there under the maple tree. It came creeping, creeping stealthily out of the valley, thinking I did not notice. And the outlines of trees and foliage nearby blended in one black mass and the night came stealing out from them, too, and from the east and west, until the only light was in the sky, filtering through the maple leaves and a star looking down through every cranny.

The night is solemn and it means mystery.

Human shapes flitted by like intangible things. Some stole up like little mice to peep at me. I did not mind. My whole being was abandoned to the soothing and penetrating charm of the night.

The katydids began their slumber song: they are at it yet. How wise they are. They do not chatter like people. They tell me only: "sleep, sleep, sleep." The wind rippled the maple leaves like little warm love thrills.

Why do fools cumber the Earth! It was a man's voice that broke the necromancer's spell. A man came to-day with his "Bible Class." He is detestable with his red cheeks and bold eyes and coarse manner and speech. What does he know of Christ? Shall I ask a young fool who was born yesterday and will die tomorrow to tell me things of Christ? I would rather ask the stars: they have seen him.

Lafcadio Hearn [1850–1904][20]

The Stranger

The Italian had kept us all spellbound for hours, while a great yellow moon was climbing higher and higher above the leaves of the bananas that nodded weirdly at the windows. Within the great hall a circle of attentive listeners—composed of that motley mixture of the wanderers of all nations, such as can be found only in New Orleans, and perhaps Marseilles—sat in silence about the lamplit table, riveted by the speaker's dark eyes and rich voice. There was a natural music in those tones; the stranger chanted as he spoke like a wizard weaving a spell. And speaking to each one in the tongue of his own land, he told them of the Orient. For he had been a wanderer in many lands; and afar off, touching the farther horn of the moonlight crescent, lay awaiting him a long, graceful vessel with a Greek name, which would unfurl her white wings for flight with the first ruddiness of morning

"I see that you are a smoker," observed the stranger to his host as he rose to go. "May I have the pleasure of presenting you with a Turkish pipe? I brought it from Constantinople."

It was moulded of blood-red clay after a fashion of Moresque art, and fretted about its edges with gilded work like the ornamentation girdling the minarets of a mosque. And a faint perfume, as of the gardens of Damascus, clung to its gaudy bowl, whereon were deeply stamped mysterious words in the Arabian tongue.

* * *

The voice had long ceased to utter its musical syllables. The guests had departed; the lamps were extinguished within. A single ray of moonlight breaking through the shrubbery without fell upon a bouquet of flowers, breathing out their perfumed souls into the night. Only the host remained—dreaming of moons larger than ours, and fiercer summers; minarets white and keen, piercing a cloudless sky, and the many-fountained pleasure-places of the East. And the pipe exhaled its strange and mystical perfume, like the scented breath of a summer's night in the rose-gardens of a Sultan. Above, in deeps of amethyst, glimmered the everlasting lamps of heaven; and from afar, the voice of a muezzin seemed to cry, in tones liquidly sweet as the voice of the stranger—"All ye who are about to sleep, commend your souls to Him who never sleeps."

Spring Phantoms

The moon, descending her staircase of clouds in one of the "Petits Poèmes en Prose," enters the chamber of a newborn child, and whispers into his dreams: "Thou shalt love all that loves me,—the water that is formless and multiform, the vast green sea, the place where thou shalt never be, the woman thou shalt never know."

For those of us thus blessed or cursed at our birth, this is perhaps the special season of such dreams—of nostalgia, vague as the world-sickness, for the places where we shall never be; and fancies as delicate as arabesques of smoke concerning the woman we shall never know. There is a languor in the air; the winds sleep; the flowers exhale their souls in incense; near sounds seem distant, as if the sense of time and space were affected by hashish; the sunsets paint in the west pictures of phantom-gold, as of those islands at the mere aspect of whose beauty crews mutinied and burned their ships; plants that droop and cling assume a more feminine grace; and the minstrel of Southern woods mingles the sweet rippling of his mocking music with the moonlight.

There have been sailors who, flung by some kind storm-wave on the shore of a Pacific Eden, to be beloved for years by some woman dark but beautiful, subsequently returned by stealth to the turmoil of civilization and labor, and vainly regretted, in the dust and roar and sunlessness of daily toil, the abandoned paradise they could never see again. Is it not such a feeling as this that haunts the mind in springtime;—a faint nostalgic longing for the place where we shall never be;—a vision made even more fairylike by such a vague dream of glory as enchanted those Spanish souls who sought and never found El Dorado?

Each time the vision returns, is it not more enchanting than before, as a recurring dream of the night in which we behold places we can never see except through dream-haze, gilded by a phantom sun? It is sadder each time, this fancy; for it brings with it the memory of older apparitions, as of places visited in childhood, in that sweet dim time so long ago that its dreams and realities are mingled together in strange confusion, as clouds with waters.

Each year it comes to haunt us, like the vision of the Adelantado of the Seven Cities,—the place where we shall never be,—and each year there will be a weirder sweetness and a more fantastic glory about the vision. And perhaps in the hours of the last beating of the heart, before sinking into that abyss of changeless deeps above whose shadowless sleep no dreams move their impalpable wings, we shall see it once more, wrapped in strange luminosity, submerged in the orange radiance of a Pacific sunset,—the place where we shall never be!

And the Woman that we shall never know!

She is the daughter of mist and light,—a phantom bride who becomes visible to us only during those magic hours when the moon enchants the world; she is the most feminine of all sweetly feminine things, the most complaisant, the least capricious. Hers is the fascination of the succubus without the red thirst of the vampire. She always wears the garb that most pleases us—when she wears any; always adopts the aspect of beauty most charming to us—blond or swarthy, Greek or Egyptian, Nubian or Circassian. She fills the place of a thousand odalisques, owns all the arts of the harem of Solomon: all the loveliness we love retrospectively, all the charms we worship in the present, are combined in her. She comes as the dead come, who never speak; yet without speech she gratifies our voiceless caprice. Sometimes we foolishly fancy that we discover in some real, warm womanly personality, a trait or feature like unto hers; but time soon unmasks our error. We shall never see her in the harsh world of realities; for she is the creation of our own hearts, wrought Pygmalionwise, but of material too unsubstantial for even the power of a god to animate. Only the dreams of Brahma himself take substantial form: these are worlds and men and all their works, which shall pass away like smoke when the preserver ceases his slumber of a myriad million years.

She becomes more beautiful as we grow older,—this phantom love, born of the mist of poor human dreams,—so fair and faultless that her invisible presence makes us less reconciled to the frailties and foibles of real life. Perhaps she too has faults; but she has no faults for us except that of unsubstantiality. Involuntarily we acquire the unjust habit of judging real women by her spectral standard; and the real always suffer for the ideal. So that when the fancy of a home and children—smiling faces, comfort, and a woman's friendship, the idea of something real to love and be loved by—comes to the haunted man in hours of disgust with the world and weariness of its hollow mockeries,—the Woman that he shall never know stands before him like a ghost with sweet sad eyes of warning,—and he dare not!

Robert Louis Stevenson [1850–1894][21]

from Fables

The Two Matches

One day there was a traveller in the woods in California, in the dry season, when the Trades were blowing strong. He had ridden a long way, and he was tired and hungry, and dismounted from his horse to smoke a pipe. But when he felt in his pocket, he found but two matches. He struck the first, and it would not light.

"Here is a pretty state of things," said the traveller. "Dying for a smoke; only one match left; and that certain to miss fire! Was there ever a creature so unfortunate? And yet," thought the traveller, "suppose I light this match, and smoke my pipe, and shake out the dottle here in the grass—the grass might catch on tire, for it is dry like tinder; and while I snatch out the flames in front, they might evade and run behind me, and seize upon yon bush of poison oak; before I could reach it, that would have blazed up; over the bush I see a pine tree hung with moss; that too would fly in fire upon the instant to its topmost bough; and the flame of that long torch—how would the trade wind take and brandish that through the inflammable forest! I hear this dell roar in a moment with the joint voice of wind and fire, I see myself gallop for my soul, and the flying conflagration chase and outflank me through the hills; I see this pleasant forest burn for days, and the cattle roasted, and the springs dried up, and the farmer ruined, and his children cast upon the world. What a world hangs upon this moment!"

With that he struck the match, and it missed fire.

"Thank God," said the traveller, and put his pipe in his pocket.

The Distinguished Stranger

Once upon a time there came to this earth a visitor from a neighbouring planet. And he was met at the place of his descent by a great philosopher, who was to show him everything.

First of all they came through a wood, and the stranger looked upon the trees. "Whom have we here?" said he.

"These are only vegetables," said the philosopher. "They are alive, but not at all interesting."

"I don't know about that," said the stranger. "They seem to have very good manners. Do they never speak ?"

"They lack the gift," said the philosopher.

"Yet I think I hear them sing," said the other.

"That is only the wind among the leaves," said the philosopher. "I will explain to you the theory of winds: it is very interesting."

"Well," said the stranger, "I wish I knew what they are thinking."

"They cannot think," said the philosopher.

I don't know about that," returned the stranger: and then laying his hand upon a trunk: "I like these people," said he.

"They are not people at all," said the philosopher. "Come along."

Next they came through a meadow where there were cows.

"These are very dirty people," said the stranger.

"They are not people at all," said the philosopher; and he explained what a cow is in scientific words which I have forgotten.

"That is all one to me," said the stranger. "But why do they never look up?"

"Because they are graminivorous," said the philosopher; "and to live upon grass, which is not highly nutritious, requires so close an attention to business that they have no time to think, or speak, or look at the scenery, or keep themselves clean."

"Well," said the stranger, "that is one way to live, no doubt. But I prefer the people with the green heads."

Next they came into a city, and the streets were full of men and women.

"These are very odd people," said the stranger.

"They are the people of the greatest nation in the world," said the philosopher.

"Are they indeed?" said the stranger. "They scarcely look so."

The Carthorses and the Saddlehorse

Two carthorses, a gelding and a mare, were brought to Samoa, and put in the same field with a saddlehorse to run free on the island. They were rather afraid to go near him, for they saw he was a saddlehorse, and supposed he would not speak to them. Now the saddlehorse had never seen creatures so big. "These must be great chiefs," thought he, and he approached them civilly. "Lady and gentleman," said he, "I understand you are from the colonies. I offer you my affectionate compliments, and make you heartily welcome to the island."

The colonials looked at him askance, and consulted with each other.

"Who can he be?" said the gelding.

"He seems suspiciously civil," said the mare.

"I do not think he can be much account," said the gelding.

"Depend upon it he is only a Kanaka," said the mare.

Then they turned to him.

"Go to the devil!" said the gelding.

"I wonder at your impudence, speaking to persons of our quality!" cried the mare.

The saddlehorse went away by himself. "I was right," said he, "they are great chiefs."

Grace King [1852–1932][22]

The Balcony

There is much of life passed on the balcony in a country where the summer unrolls in six moon-lengths, and where the nights have to come with a double endowment of vastness and splendor to compensate for the tedious, sun-parched days.

And in that country the women love to sit and talk together of summer nights, on balconies, in their vague, loose, white garments,—men are not balcony sitters,—with their sleeping children within easy hearing, the stars breaking the cool darkness, or the moon making a show of light—oh, such a discreet show of light!—through the vines. And the children inside, waking to go from one sleep into another, hear the low, soft mother-voices on the balcony, talking about this person and that, old times, old friends, old experiences; and it seems to them, hovering a moment in wakefulness, that there is no end of the world or time, or of the mother-knowledge; but illimitable as it is, the mother-voices and the mother-love and protection fill it all,— with their mother's hand in theirs, children are not afraid even of God,—and they drift into slumber again, their little dreams taking all kinds of pretty reflections from the great unknown horizon outside, as their fragile soap-bubbles take on reflections from the sun and clouds.

Experiences, reminiscences, episodes, picked up as only women know how to pick them up from other women's lives,—or other women's destinies, as they prefer to call them,—and told as only women know how to relate them; what God has done or is doing with some other woman whom they have known—that is what interests women once embarked on their own lives,—the embarkation takes place at marriage, or after the marriageable time,—or, rather, that is what interests the women who sit of summer nights on balconies. For in those long-moon countries, life is open and accessible, and romances seem to be furnished real and gratis, in order to save, in a languor-breeding climate, the ennui of reading and writing books. Each woman has a different way of picking up and relating her stories, as each one selects different pieces, and has a personal way of playing them on the piano.

Each story *is* different, or appears so to her; each has some unique and peculiar pathos in it. And so she dramatizes and inflects it, trying to make the point visible to her apparent also to her hearers. Sometimes the pathos and interest to the hearers lie only in this—that the relater has observed it, and gathered it, and finds it worth telling. For do we not gather what we have not, and is not our own lacking our one motive? It may be so, for it often appears so.

And if a child inside be wakeful and precocious, it is not dreams alone that take on reflections from the balcony outside: through the half-open shutters the still, quiet eyes look across the dim forms on the balcony to the star-spangled or the moon-brightened heavens beyond; while memory makes stores for the future, and germs are sown, out of which the slow, clambering vine of thought issues, one day, to decorate or hide, as it may be, the structures or ruins of life.

Mary E. Wilkins [1852–1930][23]

Pastels in Prose

In the Marsh-Land

Far over in the east is the marsh-land. Naught passes through it but the wind—the wind bent on strange ends—or a bird winged and swift, like a soul; but there are no souls in the marsh-land.

No foot of man sounds the deep pools; no boat cleaves the thick grasses. The pools gleam red; the grass is coarse and thick as the hair of a goat; it is flung here and there in shaggy fleeces tinged with red, as if from slaughter. Over in the east the sun stands low; his red rays color the mist like wine. The flags threaten in the wind like spears, but no heroes wield them.

There is no man in the marsh land, in whose deep pools could be found death, whose thick grasses could moor a boat forever. It is a lonely place, and only my thought is there, striving to possess it all with wide vision.

Over the marsh-land stray odors from border flowers, but there is no sense to harbor them. Over the marsh-land the sound-waves float, but there is no tongue to awaken them to speech and no ear to receive them. In the marsh-land is God, without the souls in which alone He shines unto His own vision; in the marsh-land is God, a light without His own darkness.

The marsh-land is a lonely place; there is no man there. Only my thought is there, holding what it can encompass of God.

Camilla's Snuff-Box

Here is Camilla's snuff-box.

There were shouts in the street, and the torches flared. Camilla was borne along in her sedan-chair to the rout. Her delicate yellow face, as full of fine lines as a Chinese ivory carving, was seen through the window. She wore a velvet turban, and her head nodded ever as if in a wind.

The bearers shouted; the torches flared; red flames flickered in rosy smoke. Camilla was borne along to the rout in her sedan-chair.

Camilla opened her snuff box; her slender fingers, pointed like ivory bodkins, stirred up the pungent snuff; her nostrils were as fine and fleshless as old ivory.

Camilla's time of love was past; she went to the rout with only painted roses in her cheeks, and she took a pinch of snuff.

The bearers shouted; the night was full of dark winds, which bent the red flames of the torches.

Camilla's snuff-box was of fine silver-work, and her name was on the lid. Her lover had given it to her; but her lover was long since dead, and the memory of his kisses no longer made her heart sweet.

Camilla was old, and her time of love was past. She took a pinch of snuff from her silver snuff-box, as she went to the rout in her sedan-chair, with her palsied head nodding like a Chinese toy in a cabinet.

The bearers shouted; but their shouts have long since died away. The night was full of dark winds; but the winds went down. Long ago the torches burnt out. Long ago Camilla went no more to routs, her head ceased nodding, and her funeral procession went out of sight, in a black file, down the city street. Long ago Camilla's grave was forgotten, and there was no love left for her on the earth. But here is her snuff-box.

Shadows

The black dog runs across the meadow, with his shadow at his side as fleet as he. Let him speed as he may, he cannot outspeed his shadow. There is light in the world.

It is spring. The grass is young, and the west wind blows. The banks of the brook are yellow with cowslips. The grasses all lean east when the west wind blows, and their shadows overlie them. Now the cowslips darken under a shadow. There is light in the world.

The apple-trees cast their blossoms in their dark circles of shadow. The birds fly singing overhead, and their silent shadows glide beneath them over the meadow. There is light in the world.

Half the farm-house roof glistens in the morning sun, and half is purple with shadow. The shadow of the chimney smoke floats like a cloud, over the meadow. There is light in the world.

Anne stands in the doorway. Her yellow hair and her blue gown gleam true in clear light, but she thinks of her lover, and shadows follow her thoughts. "Oh, my lover has gone on a journey! Should he lose his way! Should thieves waylay him to harm him! Should his feet falter! Should evil befall him, my lover!"

Anne stands in the doorway. Her yellow hair and her blue gown gleam true in clear light, but her thoughts cast shadows. There is love in her heart.

Death

There is a little garden full of white flowers before this house, before this little house, which is sunken in a green hillock to the lintel of its door. The white flowers are full of honey; yellow butterflies and bees suck at them. The unseen wind comes rushing like a presence and a power which the heart feels only. The white flowers press together before it in a soft tumult, and shake out fragrance like censers; but the bees and the butterflies cling to them blowing. The crickets chirp in the green roof of the house unceasingly, like clocks which have told off the past, and will tell off the future.

I pray you, friend, who dwells in this little house sunken in the green hillock, with the white flower garden before the door?

A dead man.

Passes he ever out of his little dwelling and down the path between his white flower-bushes?

He never passes out.

There is no chimney in that grassy roof. How fares he when the white flowers are gone and the white storm drives?

He feels it not.

Had he happiness?

His heart broke for it.

Does his heart pain him in there?

He has forgot.

Comes ever anybody here to visit him?

His widow comes in her black veil, and weeps here, and sometimes his old mother, wavering out in the sun like a black shadow.

And he knows it not?

He knows it not.

He knows not of his little prison-house in the green hillock, of his white flower-garden, of the winter storm, of his broken heart, and his beloved who yet bear the pain of it, and send out their thoughts to watch with him in the wintry nights?

He knows it not.

Only the living know?

Only the living.

Then, then the tombs be not for the dead, but the living! I would, I would, I would that I were dead, that I might be free from the tomb, and sorrow, and death!

Oscar Wilde [1854–1900][24]

The Artist

One evening there came into his soul the desire to fashion an image of "The Pleasure that Abideth for a Moment." And he went forth into the world to look for bronze. For he could only think in bronze.

But all the bronze of the whole world had disappeared; nor anywhere in the whole world was there any bronze to be found, save only the bronze of the image of "The Sorrow that Endureth for Ever."

Now this image he had himself, and with his own hands, fashioned, and had set on the tomb of the one thing he had loved in life. On the tomb of the dead thing he had most loved had he set this image of his own fashioning, that it might serve as a sign of the love of a man that dieth not, and a symbol of the sorrow of man that endureth forever. And in the whole world there was no other bronze save the bronze of this image.

And he took the image he had fashioned, and set it in a great furnace, and gave it to the fire.

And out of the bronze of the image of "The Sorrow that Endureth for Ever" he fashioned an image of "The Pleasure that Abideth for a Moment."

The Doer of Good

It was nighttime, and He was alone.

And He saw afar off the walls of a round city, and went towards the city.

And when He came near He heard within the city the tread of the feet of joy, and the laughter of the mouth of gladness, and the loud noise of many lutes. And He knocked at the gate and certain of the gate-keepers opened to Him.

And He beheld a house that was of marble, and had fair pillars of marble before it. The pillars were hung with garlands, and within and without there were torches of cedar. And He entered the house.

And when He had passed through the hall of chalcedony and the hall of jasper, and reached the long hall of feasting, He saw lying on a couch of sea-purple one whose hair was crowned with red roses and whose lips were red with wine.

And He went behind him and touched him on the shoulder, and said to him:

"Why do you live like this?"

And the young man turned round and recognised Him, and made answer, and said: "But I was a leper once, and you healed me. How else should I live?"

And He passed out of the house and went again into the street.

And after a little while He saw one whose face and raiment were painted and whose feet were shod with pearls. And behind her came slowly, as a hunter, a young man who wore a cloak of two colors. Now the face of the woman was as the fair face of an idol, and the eyes of the young man were bright with lust.

And He followed swiftly, and touched the hand of the young man, and said to him: "Why do you look at this woman and in such wise?"

And the young man turned round and recognised Him, and said: "But I was blind once, and you gave me sight. At what else should I look?"

And He ran forward and touched the painted raiment of the woman, and said to her: "Is there no other way in which to walk save the way of sin?"

And the woman turned round and recognised Him, and laughed, and said: "But you forgave me my sins, and the way is a pleasant way."

And He passed out of the city.

And when He had passed out of the city, He saw, seated by the roadside, a young man who was weeping.

And He went towards him and touched the long locks of his hair, and said to him: "Why are you weeping?"

And the young man looked up and recognised Him, and made answer: "But I was dead once, and you raised me from the dead. What else should I do but weep?"

The Disciple

When Narcissus died, the pool of his pleasure changed from a cup of sweet waters into a cup of salt tears, and the Oreads came weeping through the woodland that they might sing to the pool and give it comfort.

And when they saw that the pool had changed from a cup of sweet waters into a cup of salt tears, they loosened the green tresses of their hair, and cried to the pool, and said: "We do not wonder that you should mourn in this manner for Narcissus, so beautiful was he."

"But was Narcissus beautiful?" said the pool.

"Who should know better than you?" answered the Oreads. "Us did he ever pass by, but you he sought for, and would lie on your banks and look down at you, and in the mirror of your waters he would mirror his own beauty."

And the pool answered: "But I loved Narcissus because, as he lay on my banks and looked down at me, in the mirror of his eyes I saw my own beauty mirrored."

Olive Schreiner [1855–1920][25]

from Dreams

The Gardens of Pleasure

She walked upon the beds, and the sweet rich scent arose; and she gathered her hands full of flowers. Then Duty, with his white clear features, came and looked at her. Then she ceased from gathering, but she walked away among the flowers, smiling, and with her hands full.

Then Duty, with his still white face, came again, and looked at her; but she, she turned her head away from him. At last she saw his face, and she dropped the fairest of the flowers she had held, and walked silently away.

Then again he came to her. And she moaned, and bent her head low, and turned to the gate. But as she went out she looked back at the sunlight on the faces of the flowers, and wept in anguish. Then she went out, and it shut behind her for ever; but still in her hand she held of the buds she had gathered, and the scent was very sweet in the lonely desert.

But he followed her. Once more he stood before her with his still, white, death-like face. And she knew what he had come for: she unbent the fingers, and let the flowers drop out, the flowers she had loved so, and walked on without them, with dry, aching eyes. Then for the last time he came. And she showed him her empty hands, the hands that held nothing now. But still he looked. Then at length she opened her bosom and took out of it one small flower she had hidden there, and laid it on the sand. She had nothing more to give now, and she wandered away, and the grey sand whirled about her.

Life's Gifts

I saw a woman sleeping. In her sleep she dreamt Life stood before her, and held in each hand a gift—in the one Love, in the other Freedom. And she said to the woman, "Choose!"

And the woman waited long: and she said, "Freedom!"

And Life said, "Thou hast well chosen. If thou hadst said, 'Love,' I would have given thee that thou didst ask for; and I would have gone from thee, and returned to thee no more. Now, the day will come when I shall return. In that day I shall bear both gifts in one hand."

I heard the woman laugh in her sleep.

The Artists's Secret

There was an artist once, and he painted a picture. Other artists had colours richer and rarer, and painted more notable pictures. He painted his with one color, there was a wonderful red glow on it; and the people went up and down, saying, "We like the picture, we like the glow."

The other artists came and said, "Where does he get his color from?" They asked him; and he smiled and said, "I cannot tell you"; and worked on with his head bent low.

And one went to the far East and bought costly pigments, and made a rare color and painted, but after a time the picture faded. Another read in the old books, and made a color rich and rare, but when he had put it on the picture it was dead.

But the artist painted on. Always the work got redder and redder, and the artist grew whiter and whiter. At last one day they found him dead before his picture, and they took him up to bury him. The other men looked about in all the pots and crucibles, but they found nothing they had not.

And when they undressed him to put his grave-clothes on him, they found above his left breast the mark of a wound—it was an old, old wound, that must have been there all his life, for the edges were old and hardened; but Death, who seals all things, had drawn the edges together, and closed it up.

And they buried him. And still the people went about saying, "Where did he find his color from?" And it came to pass that after a while the artist was forgotten—but the work lived.

Fiona Macleod [William Sharp, 1855–1905][26]

from THE SILENCE OF AMOR

NOCTURNE

By dim, mauve and dream-white bushes of lilac I pass to the cypress alley, and to the mere which lies breathless in the moon-shine. A fish leaps, a momentary flame of fire. Then all is still again on the moonlit mere, where, breathless, it lies beyond the cypress alley. In the vague moonshine of the cypress alley I pass again, a silent shadow, by the dim, mauve and dream-white bushes of lilac.

THE NIGHTJAR

Low upon a pine-branch a nightjar leans and sings his churring song. He sings his churring song to his mate, who, poised upon a juniper hard by, listens with quivering wings.

The whirring of the nightjar fills the dusk, heavy with the fragrance of new-mown hay. There is neither star nor moon in the dim, flowing darkness, only the red and yellow wayfaring flames where the glow-worms are. Like a wandering wave, in the dewy dark, the churring note of the nightjar rises and falls against the juniper bush hard by.

HIGH NOON

To-day, as I walked at high noon, listening to the larks filling the April blue with a spray of delicate song, I saw a shadow pass me, where no one was, and where nothing moved, above me or around. It was not my shadow that passed me, nor the shadow of one for whom I longed. That other shadow came not.

I have heard that there is a god clothed in shadow who goes to and fro among the human kind, putting silence between hearts with his waving hands, and breathing a chill out of his cold breath, and leaving a gulf as of deep waters flowing between them because of the passing of his feet.

Thus, thus it was that that other shadow for which I longed came not. Yet, in the April blue I heard the wild aerial chimes of song, and watched the golden fulfillment of the day under the high illimitable arch of noon.

The White Procession

One by one the stars come forth—solemn eyes watching for ever the white procession move onward orderly where there is neither height, nor depth, nor beginning, nor end.

In the vast stellar space the moonglow wanes until it grows cold, white, ineffably remote. Only upon our little dusky earth, upon our restless span of waters, the light descends in a tender warmth.

Deep gladness to me, though but the creature of an hour, that I am on this little moonlit dusky earth. Too cold, too white, too ineffably remote the moonglow in these vast wastes of Infinity where, one by one, the constellations roam—solemn witnesses watching for ever the white procession move onward orderly where there is neither height, nor depth, nor beginning, nor end.

Alcée Fortier, trans. [1856–1914][27]

The Tortoise [Tortie]

A gentleman who was living on the banks of a bayou caught a large tortoise, and went immediately to invite some friends to take dinner with him. His little boy, in his absence, went to the cage where was the tortoise, and the latter began to whistle. "How well you whistle!" said the child. "Oh! that is nothing; open the cage, and you will see." The boy opened the cage, and the tortoise whistled better than ever. The boy was delighted. "Put me down on the floor and you will see," said the tortoise. The boy did so, and the tortoise danced and sang. "Oh! how well you dance and sing!" said the boy. "Put me on the bank of the bayou, and you will see," said the tortoise. The boy took her to the bayou, and the tortoise danced and sang. All at once she disappeared in the water, and the boy began to cry. The tortoise rose in the middle of the bayou and said: "Learn not to trust, hereafter, people whom you do not know."

The boy was afraid of his father, and put a large flat stone into the cage. The cook, thinking it was the tortoise, put the stone into the kettle. She was astonished to see it remain hard so long, and she called her master's attention to it. He ordered the tortoise to be put upon the table, and he took his table knife to cut it. It was in vain. He took the carving-knife, in vain. He took the hatchet, in vain. He took the axe, he broke the dishes, the table, but the tortoise remained intact. He then saw it was a stone, and to this day he has not understood how his tortoise was changed into a stone.

The Devil's Marriage [Mariaze Djabe]

One day there was a pretty young girl, but she was very proud, and every time the young men came to court her, she found a pretext to send them away. One was too small, another was too tall, another had red hair; in short, she refused all her suitors. One day her mother said to her: "My daughter, you see that tall, tall tree in the middle of the river? I am going to put this pumpkin on the smallest branch at the top of the tree, and that young man who will be able to climb up and catch the pumpkin will be your husband."

The daughter said she had no objection, so they put a notice in the newspapers. The next week a crowd of young men presented themselves, and among them one who was beautifully dressed and exceedingly handsome. He was the Devil, but nobody knew him. The young girl told her mother: "I wish he would catch the pumpkin."

All the young men climbed on the tree, but no one could succeed in reaching the pumpkin. When the turn of the Devil came, in one minute he was up the tree, and had the pumpkin in his hand. As soon as he was down he said to the young girl: "Come now, come with me to my house."

The girl put on her best dress and went away with the Devil. On the road they met a man, who said to the Devil: "Give me my cravat and my collar which I had lent to you."

The Devil took off his cravat and his collar, and said: "Here, take your old cravat and your old collar." A little further on, another man saw the Devil and told him: "Give me my shirt which I had lent you." The Devil took off his shirt and said: "Here, here, take your old shirt." A little further, he saw another man, who said to him: "Give me my cloak which I had lent to you." The Devil took off his cloak, and said: "Here, here, take your old cloak." A little further, another man asked for his trousers, then another one for his hat. The Devil took off the trousers and the hat, and said: "Here, here, take your old trousers and your old hat." He came down from his carriage and disappeared for a few minutes, then he returned as well dressed as before.

The young lady was beginning to be very much frightened when they met another man, who said: "Give me my horses which I had lent to you." The Devil gave him his four horses, and said to his wife: "Get down from the carriage and hitch yourself to it." She drew the carriage as far as the Devil's house, and was so frightened that her heart was almost in her mouth.

The Devil entered his garden, and said to his wife: "Remain here with my mother." As soon as he was gone the mother said to the young lady: "Ah! my daughter, you have taken a bad husband; you have married the Devil."

The poor girl was so sorry that she did not know what to do, and she said to the old woman: "Can you not tell me how I can run away?" The old woman replied: "Yes, wait until to-morrow morning; but come, let me show you something." She opened the door of a little room, and said: "Look, my daughter." The girl looked in the room, and what did she see? A number of women hanging from a nail. She was so frightened that she asked the old woman if she could not hide her somewhere until the next morning. The woman said: "Yes, but let me tell you how you can escape from here. When the Devil tells you to give one sack of corn to his rooster which wakes him up in the morning, you will give him three sacks that he may eat more and not crow so early. Then you will go to the chicken house and take six dirty eggs. Take care not to take clean eggs; that will bring you bad luck."

The next morning the young lady gave the rooster three sacks of corn, she took her eggs, and ran away. When the rooster had finished eating his three sacks, he crowed: "Mr. Devil, awake quickly; some one has run away from the house!" The Devil got up quickly and started running after his wife. The poor girl looked behind her, and saw smoke and fire—indeed, the Devil himself. She took an egg and broke it: a high wooden fence arose in the middle of the road. The Devil had to return home to get his golden axe to cut down the fence. After he had broken down the fence he took his axe to his house.

The girl looked behind her; she saw smoke and fire—the Devil himself. She broke another egg: there grew up an iron fence. The Devil went home to get his golden axe, and had to take it back after breaking the fence.

The girl looked again; there was fire and smoke. She broke another egg: a great fire rose up in the road. The Devil went to get his jar of water to put out the fire, and then had to take the jar back.

The girl heard again a noise; it was fire and smoke. She broke another egg: a brick wall grew up. The Devil went to get his golden axe, and carried it back after breaking the wall.

The girl looked again: she saw fire and smoke. She broke another egg: a small river appeared, in which was a small canoe. She entered the canoe and crossed the river. The Devil was obliged to swim across.

The girl looked again; she saw fire and smoke. She broke another egg: a large river appeared. There was a big crocodile on the other side of the river warming himself in the sun. The girl sang: "Grandmother, I pray you, cross me over; grandmother, I pray you, save my life." The crocodile said : "Climb on my back, my little one, I shall save your life."

The Devil saw in what way the girl had crossed the river, so he said to the crocodile: "Cross me over, crocodile; cross me over." The crocodile replied: "Climb on my back; I shall cross you over." When he reached the middle of the river, he dived under the water, and the Devil was drowned.

When the girl had left her mother's house with her husband, her mother had said to her: "Well, my child, what do you wish me to do with your old white horse?" The girl said to her mother: "I don't care what you do; put him out in the pasture and let him die if he wants to." However, when she crossed the river on the crocodile's back, she saw her old horse in the pasture, and she said to him: "I pray you, old body, save my life!" The horse replied: "Ah, you want me now to save your life; did you not tell your mother to let me die, if I wanted? Well, climb on my back, I shall carry you to your mother."

The girl soon reached her mother's house. She got down from the horse and kissed him, then she kissed her mother. She remained at home after that, and did not wish to marry again, after having had the Devil for her husband.

James Gibbons Huneker [1857–1921][28]

Nuptials Royal

She lay in the Hall of the Mirrors where, repeated in evanescent gestures, her person moved with processional precision. She had disrobed to the accompaniment of soft, hidden music, and to the unconscious miming of the mirrors; something of fear and something of shame were in her heart as she pulled to her pretty chin the royal counterpane. It was the first time she had ever lain in a palace, and the night seemed to hum with a thousand harps. It was the music and the beating of het heart that she heard, and she wondered most at the heavily scented atmosphere, and smiled at the face that smiled down at her from the shining ceiling. Her plump body sank in relaxing curves; the very couch seemed to embrace her. Then she heard footsteps and dared no longer gaze into the ironic mirror overhead. As the prince approached love loomed nigh. There was no tenderness in his eyes, and his young forehead was slightly wrinkled. It was his nuptial night; for him was waiting a fair girl, whose pulses leapt to the sound of his voice. But he had no words for her when he reached the royal bed that stood in the Hall of the Mirrors. His troubled gaze drove the blood to her heart, when he sat beside her and the music ceased and the mirrors grew grey and misty. She had waited for this moment since her birth; their souls had been woven together by imperial decree, yet now they circled about each other like two tall stars in interstellar depths, bound for eternity to tread in the stately dance of the spheres, eons apart, and destined never to embrace. With outstretched, despairing arms she welcomed her image in the air above her, and her impassioned, sorrowful glance married her to her own soul. The prince told her in falsetto tones of his desire for rest, and she welcomed him as one would a pet poodle; beside his sleepy escaping soul she lay in the Hall of the Mirrors, where, repeated in evanescent gestures, her person moved in processional sadness.

Mary Alicia Owen, compiler [1858–1935][29]

How the Skunk Became the Terror of All Living Creatures

Skunk was Catamount's young brother. He was a disgrace to the family from the day he was born. He was sneaking, he was cowardly. He was thievish too, for that matter. He thought more of getting at a bird's nest and stealing a few half-rotten eggs than of seeking and overpowering worthy prey. He gave his strength to catching field-mice and even grasshoppers and locusts. Even gophers and moles despised more than they feared him. Added to this, he was the most impertinent and insulting little beast that could be imagined when he was in a safe place and could call to those whom he wished to affront from a distance. He even showed disrespect to Grey Wolf.

This was not to be tolerated, so Grey Wolf called all the animals together and demanded to know what should be done. With one voice, the answer came—

"Destroy him. He is of no use whatever."

Now Catamount and Black Wolf said nothing. Catamount could not excuse and would not condemn his brother. Black Wolf had plans of his own for the culprit to carry out.

Grey Wolf, thinking that all were agreed, was about to destroy the miserable skunk, but the contemptible creature flattened himself out at the feet of his master and entreated that the boon of life might be spared him, no matter if all that adorned and made it pleasant be taken away. So in contempt, rather than kindness, Grey Wolf spared the life of Skunk, but at the same time he shrunk and shrivelled the creature till he was scarcely larger than Gopher. He pared his claws and shortened his teeth. This done, the other animals scornfully departed without taking leave, Catamount going next after Grey Wolf.

Black Wolf had only gone a little way when he turned and went softly back.

"Be of good cheer, little brother," he said to the dismayed Skunk. "Brother Grey Wolf has seen fit to arrange matters so that you shall be in terror of all things breathing. Now, I come to put all things, even Grey Wolf himself in awe of you."

This he promised, not because he loved Skunk, but because it delighted him to thwart the intentions of Grey Wolf.

Then Skunk lifted up his head and thanked Black Wolf, and asked—

"What can you do? My strength is gone, my claws are as grass and my teeth as willow-twigs."

"Watch me," said Black Wolf.

So Skunk watched and saw Black Wolf take an egg from a deserted nest and put in it sweat from his own body, the breath of a buzzard, wind that had passed over the field where the dead still lay after the battle, and a little water from a green pool. When he had stirred these things together, he gave the egg to Skunk and said—

"Wear this, and you shall be the great conqueror. Your strongest antagonists shall turn sickly and feeble before you. Not horns, claws, teeth, sinews, or bulk shall make any difference to you."

So Skunk took the gift with a joyful heart and tried its power on Black Wolf at once.

Black Wolf, sick and howling, fled as fast as he was able from the presence of the ungrateful Skunk he had so terribly endowed.

Then Skunk knew for a certainty that Black Wolf had told him the truth about the gift, so he set out to find his revilers and drive them before him. When he found them, they fled, every one, from least to greatest.

Then Skunk contentedly laid himself down under a tree and went to sleep.

Charlotte Perkins Gilman [1860–1935][30]

An Extinct Angel

There was once a species of angel inhabiting this planet, acting as "a universal solvent" to all the jarring, irreconcilable elements of human life.

It was quite numerous; almost every family had one; and, although differing in degree of seraphic virtue, all were, by common consent, angels.

The advantages of possessing such a creature were untold. In the first place, the chances of the mere human being in the way of getting to heaven were greatly increased by these semi-heavenly belongings; they gave one a sort of lien on the next world, a practical claim most comforting to the owner.

For the angels of course possessed virtues above mere humanity; and because the angels were so well-behaved, therefore the owners were given credit.

Beside this direct advantage of complimentary tickets up above were innumerable indirect advantages below. The possession of one of these angels smoothed every feature of life, and gave peace and joy to an otherwise hard lot.

It was the business of the angel to assuage, to soothe, to comfort, to delight. No matter how unruly were the passions of the owner, sometimes even to the extent of legally beating his angel with "a stick no thicker than his thumb," the angel was to have no passion whatever—unless self-sacrifice may be called a passion, and indeed it often amounted to one with her.

The human creature went out to his daily toil and comforted himself as he saw fit. He was apt to come home tired and cross, and in this exigency it was the business of the angel to wear a smile for his benefit—a soft, perennial, heavenly smile.

By an unfortunate limitation of humanity the angel was required, in addition to such celestial duties as smiling and soothing, to do kitchen service, cleaning, sewing, nursing, and other mundane tasks. But these things must be accomplished without the slightest diminution of the angelic virtues.

The angelic virtues, by the way, were of a curiously paradoxical nature.

They were inherent. A human being did not pretend to name them, could not be expected to have them, acknowledged them as far beyond his gross earthly nature; and yet, for all this, he kept constant watch over the virtues of the angel, wrote whole books of advice for angels on how they should behave, and openly held that angels would lose their virtues altogether should they once cease to obey the will and defer to the judgment of human kind.

This looks strange to us to-day as we consider these past conditions, but then it seemed fair enough; and the angels—bless their submissive, patient hearts!—never thought of questioning it.

It was perhaps only to be expected that when an angel fell the human creature should punish the celestial creature with unrelenting fury. It was so much easier to be an angel than to be human, that there was no excuse for an angel's falling, even by means of her own angelic pity and tender affection.

It seems perhaps hard that the very human creature the angel fell on, or fell with, or fell to—however you choose to put it—was as harsh as anyone in condemnation of the fall. He never assisted the angel to rise, but got out from under and resumed his way, leaving her in the mud. She was a great convenience to walk on, and, as was stoutly maintained by the human creature, helped keep the other angels clean.

This is exceedingly mysterious, and had better not be inquired into too closely.

The amount of physical labor of a severe and degrading sort required of one of these bright spirits, was amazing. Certain kinds of work—always and essentially dirty—were relegated wholly to her. Yet one of her first and most rigid duties was the keeping of her angelic robes spotlessly clean.

The human creature took great delight in contemplating the flowing robes of the angels. Their changeful motion suggested to him all manner of sweet and lovely thoughts and memories; also, the angelic virtues above mentioned were supposed largely to inhere in the flowing robes. Therefore flow they must, and the ample garments waved unchecked over the weary limbs of the wearer, the contiguous furniture and the stairs. For the angels unfortunately had no wings, and their work was such as required a good deal of going up and down stairs.

It is quite a peculiar thing, in contemplating this work, to see how largely it consisted in dealing with dirt. Yes, it does seem strange to this enlightened age; but the fact was that the angels waited on the human creatures in every form of menial service, doing things as their natural duty which the human creature loathed and scorned.

It does seem irreconcilable, but they reconciled it. The angel was an angel and the work was the angel's work, and what more do you want?

There is one thing about the subject which looks a little suspicious: The angels—I say it under breath—were not very bright!

The human creatures did not like intelligent angels—intelligence seemed to dim their shine, somehow, and pale their virtues. It was harder to reconcile things where the angels had any sense. Therefore every possible care was taken to prevent the angels from learning anything of our gross human wisdom.

But little by little, owing to the unthought-of consequences of repeated intermarriage between the angel and the human being, the angel longed for, found and ate the fruit of the forbidden tree of knowledge.

And in that day she surely died.

The species is now extinct. It is rumored that here and there in remote regions you can still find a solitary specimen—in places where no access is to be had to the deadly fruit; but the race as a race is extinct.

Poor dodo!

Deserted

Mrs. Ellphalet Johnson was a very hardworking woman—even her next door neighbors admitted that. Her chimney blackened the soft morning air as early as any in town; her wash fluttered white under the apple boughs long before breakfast. That is, before Ellphalet's breakfast.

Ellphalet kept store. He preferred keeping store to farming because he could sit down more. In the store it was all in the way of business. His customers sat down on every available object—the counter, the sugar barrel, the cracker box, even the cask of molasses, but not on that last until the counter and other things were full.

There were a few chairs around the store in the rear and vast political measures were discussed there—matters far beyond the reach of Mrs. Johnson's busy feminine brain.

The house was over the store. The stairs connecting the two came down in the end where the store was, and when a customer came in who wanted not a seat but service Mr. Ellphalet Johnson would tip back his chair a little further, open the stair door and say, "Maria!"

Then Mrs. Johnson would hurry down and attend to the customer. Mrs. Johnson had a good head in a servile sort of way and usually kept the accounts. This she did after the store was closed and the children were in bed.

But in spite of all her efforts Ellphalet got into difficulties. He never fully explained to her what these difficulties were, but they were such as induced him to transfer the family bank account and business liabilities to her name.

This, he explained with lofty comprehensiveness, was merely a matter of form, and quite essential for the safety of the children.

"And Maria," he added, seeking to bring the conversation to a more comprehensible level, "there's a lady over at Clark's, a Miss Burton, who wants board in a private family, and I told her she could come here. I knew the spare room was suitable, and one more or less wouldn't make any difference to you."

"But I wanted mother for a while this summer!" urged Maria. "She'd be such a help preservin' and with the baby."

Ellphalet grinned.

"Well, I don't want your mother," said he: "not by a long chalk. And this lady is to pay a dollar a day right along and you're to bank it in your name—here's the book."

Maria took the book and looked at it. Eight hundred dollars were set down already to her credit.

"Why, 'Liphalet. Where'd you get this?" she exclaimed.

"Sold the river lot," he answered, and tipped back his chair to its farthest, looking at her with narrowed eyes from under the brim of his hat.

A dull red color rose on Mrs. Johnson's faded face.

"That was my lot," said she slowly. "My father gave it to me when he died and I never meant to have had it sold in the world."

"You don't know nothin' about business an' never will," said Ellphalet. But now you pay 'tention to this and see if you can understand it. Here's the deeds of this house, store an' all the furniture and stock. All in your name. Now. The reason of it is that I've got creditors who might clean me out any time, but if I can tide over this year I'll get over it all right. For this year the hull property's in your name and none of my creditors can touch it. See? As to that lot 'twan't no more yours than this house was or the farm—they all come from your father, but when you married me it made 'em mine, and it ought to. A man supports the family. He's got to hold the property. But for this year it's in your name."

The year passed slowly. Mrs. Johnson grew to understand somewhat of the value of her position and to do more and more of the business.

In truth, though she never owned to her most intimate friend that "'Liphalet drinked!" this sad fact was now becoming painfully apparent.

Much had Mrs. Johnson suffered in the fifteen years of her laborious marriage. She had worked, on the average, fifteen hours a day, and lost much sleep besides. She had put into the family all its real estate, and really kept the store. She had borne and reared four children and lost two, and out of all this she had learned nothing until what she thought the last straw turned out to be a blessing in disguise. That was the lady boarder. If Mr. Johnson had dreamed of that worthy woman's real position he would never have placed his conservative spare chamber at her disposal.

But he did not suspect, and never learned until it was too late.

She was a lawyer, and in spite of the absolute prohibition of all brain work for three months, she had brought with her a few little calf-bound books from force of habit.

So it chanced that Mrs. Johnson, in the invigorating freshness of new acquaintance, was led to read somewhat in the penal and civil codes of her native State. Moreover, the boarder, moved by a strong sense of human kindness to this struggling woman and seeing the responsibilities of life with wider reach, urged upon her a new view of her duties to her children and the world.

Wherefore, it came to pass that when Ellphalet waked up one morning very late, indeed, after a little heavier drinking than was usual to him, and called vainly, with quite advanced profanity, for his faithful wife, he found her not in attendance.

Somewhat sobered by surprise he arose and searched the house.

No wife, no child, no boarder!

And a little later, to his incredulous horror and amazement, he discovered that the house and store, stock, furniture and farm had been sold over his head, and the proceeds had disappeared with his wife.

She left him a letter, however, in which it was set forth that if he gave up drinking and became a self-supporting citizen she would gladly receive him again as a husband—on her own terms.

In the meantime she would allow him $30 a month, to be paid to him personally on application to her lawyer, whose address she enclosed.

For herself she had gore into business independently, and should do well by the children.

Ellphalet read the letter repeatedly.

The name of the lawyer confused him.

"Elizabeth!" said he. "Elizabeth Burton! Great Scott!"

Then the deserted husband took up the burden of life. It made a new man of him.

Prisons for Animals

Spring is in the air. All creatures feel it. The fish are shooting up the rivers, the birds hard working and happy; every animal feels the lift and stir and new life. Even those which are in prison. . . .

What excuse has the Prison for Animals? What have they done to merit this life sentence?

Spring is in the air. The trees are misty with soft color, blurred with swelling buds, all aslant with curly tassels of young blossoms. The grass is pushing up in joyous vigor, green as it is never green again; soft, sweet, the delicious new first growth; beginning of a long summer's feasting.

Here are the deer prisons. They have a high iron fence around them, another railing outside that. They have a wooden house for shelter. They have underfoot, cinders—gravel and cinders. . . .

To keep in a prison yard an animal built for speed, accustomed to wide ranging, to long swift flight, is cruelty. . . .

And for what? For whose benefit? Does it give pleasure? Those who find pleasure in gazing at helpless pain had better go unpleased. . . .

These beasts in prison, these who bear no burdens, provide neither food nor drink, wool nor hide—what excuse have we for tormenting them?

Here is a bald eagle. A bird of freedom. . . . The eagle sits huddled, dull as a brooding vulture. . . .

Here is a hawk, fierce-eyed. He beats his wings to tatters . . . against the bars.

Here is an elephant, huge, patient, with small, smouldering eyes that see more than we think. Manacled, this beast, chained at both ends, fore foot and hind foot, to stout posts. The elephant is a water lover. His dry hide itches for water. He wants to wade into it, to draw it up and pour it all over himself. . . .

All wild creatures have a keen, delicate sense of smell. . . . We imprison them in fetid odors. They needs must breathe, night and day, the repulsive smell of their enemies, odors of danger and distrust. . . .

Those who work for the humane education of the young, recommend that humanely disposed people discourage the caging of animals and withdraw their patronage from all such exhibitions.

Edith Wharton [1862–1937][31]

The Valley of Childish Things, and Other Emblems

I.

Once upon a time a number of children lived together in the Valley of Childish Things, playing all manner of delightful games, and studying the same lesson-books. But one day a little girl, one of their number, decided that it was time to see something of the world about which the lesson-books had taught her; and as none of the other children cared to leave their games, she set out alone to climb the pass which led out of the valley.

It was a hard climb, but at length she reached a cold, bleak table-land beyond the mountains. Here she saw cities and men, and learned many useful arts, and in so doing grew to be a woman. But the table-land was bleak and cold, and when she had served her apprenticeship she decided to return to her old companions in the Valley of Childish Things, and work with them instead of with strangers.

It was a weary way back, and her feet were bruised by the stones, and her face was beaten by the weather; but half way down the pass she met a man, who kindly helped her over the roughest places. Like herself, he was lame and weather-beaten; but as soon as he spoke she recognized him as one of her old playmates. He too had been out in the world, and was going back to the valley; and on the way they talked together of the work they meant to do there. He had been a dull boy, and she had never taken much notice of him; but as she listened to his plans for building bridges and draining swamps and cutting roads through the jungle, she thought to herself, "Since he has grown into such a fine fellow, what splendid men and women my other playmates must have become!"

But what was her surprise to find, on reaching the valley, that her former companions, instead of growing into men and women, had all remained little children. Most of them were playing the same old games, and the few who affected to be working were engaged in such strenuous occupations as building mudpies and sailing paper boats in basins. As for the lad who had been the favorite companion of her studies, he was playing marbles with all the youngest boys in the valley.

At first the children seemed glad to have her back, but soon she saw that her presence interfered with their games; and when she tried to tell them of the great things that were being done on the table-land beyond the mountains, they picked up their toys and went farther down the valley to play.

Then she turned to her fellow-traveler, who was the only grown man in the valley; but he was on his knees before a dear little girl with blue eyes and a coral necklace, for whom he was making a garden out of cockle-shells and bits of glass, and broken flowers stuck in sand.

The little girl was clapping her hands and crowing (she was too young to speak articulately); and when she who had grown to be a woman laid her hand on the man's shoulder, and asked him if he did not want to set to work with her building bridges, draining swamps, and cutting roads through the jungle, he replied that at that particular moment he was too busy.

And as she turned away, he added in the kindest possible way, "Really, my dear, you ought to have taken better care of your complexion."

II.

There was once a maiden lady who lived alone in a conmodious brick house facing north and south. The lady was very fond of warmth and sunshine, but unfortunately her room was on the north side of the house, so that in winter she had no sun at all.

This distressed her so much that, after long deliberation, she sent for an architect, and asked him if it would be possible to turn the house around so that her room should face the south. The architect replied that anything could be done for money, but the estimated cost of turning the house around was so high that the lady, who enjoyed a handsome income, was obliged to reduce her way of living and sell her securities at a sacrifice to raise money enough for the purpose.

At length, however, the house was turned around, and she felt almost consoled for her impoverishment by the first ray of sunlight which stole through her shutters the next morning.

That very day she received a visit from an old friend who had been absent a year; and this friend, finding her seated at her window in a flood of sunlight, immediately exclaimed:

"My dear, how sensible of you to have moved into a south room! I never could understand why you persisted so long in living on the north side of the house."

And the following day the architect sent in his bill.

III.

There was once a little girl who was so very intelligent that her parents feared that she would die.

But an aged aunt, who had crossed the Atlantic in a sailing-vessel, said, "My dears, let her marry the first man she falls in love with, and she will make such a fool of herself that it will probably save her life."

IV.

A thinly clad man, who was trudging afoot through a wintry and shelterless region, met another wrapped in a big black cloak. The cloak hung heavily on its wearer, and seemed to drag him back, but at least it kept off the cold.

"That 's a fine warm cloak you've got," said the first man through his chattering teeth.

"Oh," said the other, "it's none of my choosing, I promise you. It's only my old happiness dyed black and made over into a sorrow; but in this weather a man must wear what he's got."

"To think of some people's luck!" muttered the first man, as the other passed on. "Now I never had enough happiness to make a sorrow out of."

V.

There was once a man who married a sweet little wife; but when he set out with her from her father's house, he found that she had never been taught to walk. They had a long way to go, and there was nothing for him to do but to carry her; and as he carried her she grew heavier and heavier.

Then they came to a wide, deep river, and he found that she had never been taught to swim. So he told her to hold fast to his shoulder, and started to swim with her across the river. And as he swam she grew frightened, and dragged him down in her struggles. And the river was deep and wide, and the current ran fast; and once or twice she nearly had him under. But he fought his way through, and landed her safely on the other side; and behold, he found himself in a strange country, beyond all imagining delightful. And as he looked about him and gave thanks, he said to himself:

"Perhaps if I hadn't had to carry her over, I shouldn't have kept up long enough to get here myself."

VI.

A soul once cowered in a gray waste, and a mighty shape came by. Then the soul cried out for help, saying, "Shall I be left to perish alone in this desert of Unsatisfied Desires?"

"But you are mistaken," the shape replied; "this is the land of Gratified Longings. And, moreover, you are not alone, for the country is full of people; but whoever tarries here grows blind."

VII.

There was once a very successful architect who made a great name for himself. At length he built a magnificent temple, to which he devoted more time and thought than to any of the other buildings he had erected; and the world pronounced it his masterpiece. Shortly afterward he died, and when he came before the judgment angel he was not asked how many sins he had committed, but how many houses he had built.

He hung his head and said, more than he could count.

The judgment angel asked what they were like, and the architect said that he was afraid they were pretty bad.

"And are you sorry?" asked the angel.

"Very sorry," said the architect, with honest contrition.

"And how about that famous temple that you built just before you died?" the angel continued. "Are you satisfied with that?"

"Oh, no," the architect exclaimed. "I really think it has some good points about it,—I did try my best, you know,—but there's one dreadful mistake that I'd give my soul to go back and rectify."

"Well," said the angel, "you can't go back and rectify it, but you can take your choice of the following alternatives: either we can let the world go on thinking your temple a masterpiece and you the greatest architect that ever lived, or we can send to earth a young fellow we've got here who will discover your mistake at a glance, and point it out so clearly to posterity that you'll be the laughing-stock of all succeeding generations of architects. Which do you choose?"

"Oh, well," said the architect, "if it comes to that, you know—as long as it suits my clients as it is, I really don't see the use of making such a fuss."

VIII.

A man once married a charming young person who agreed with him on every question. At first they were very happy, for the man thought his wife the most interesting companion he had ever met, and they spent their days telling each other what wonderful people they were. But by and by the man began to find his wife rather tiresome. Wherever he went she insisted upon going; whatever he did, she was sure to tell him that it would have been better to do the opposite; and moreover, it gradually dawned upon him that his friends had never thought so highly of her as he did. Having made this discovery, he naturally felt justified in regarding himself as the aggrieved party; she took the same view of her situation, and their life was one of incessant recrimination.

Finally, after years spent in violent quarrels and short-lived reconciliations, the man grew weary, and decided to divorce his wife.

He engaged an able lawyer, who assured him that he would have no difficulty in obtaining a divorce; but to his surprise, the judge refused to grant it.

"But—" said the man, and he began to recapitulate his injuries.

"That's all very true," said the judge, "and nothing would be easier than for you to obtain a divorce if you had only married another person."

"What do you mean by another person?" asked the man in astonishment.

"Well," replied the judge, "it appears that you inadvertently married yourself; that is a union no court has the power to dissolve."

"Oh," said the man; and he was secretly glad, for in his heart he was already longing to make it up again with his wife.

IX.

There was once a gentleman who greatly disliked to assume any responsibility. Being possessed of ample means and numerous poor relatives, he might have indulged a variety of tastes and even a few virtues; but since there is no occupation that does not bring a few cares in its train, this gentleman resolutely refrained from doing anything.

He ceased to visit his old mother, who lived in the country, because it made him nervous to catch the train; he subscribed to no charities because it was a bother to write the checks; he received no visits because he did not wish to be under the obligation of returning them; he invited no guests to stay with him, for fear of being bored before they left; he gave no presents because it was so troublesome to choose them; finally, he even gave up asking his friends to dine because it was such a nuisance to tell the cook that they were coming.

This gentleman took an honest pride in his complete detachment from the trivial importunities of life, and was never tired of ridiculing those who complained of the weight of their responsibilities, justly remarking that if they really wished to be their own masters they had only to follow his example.

One day, however, one of his servants carelessly left the front door open, and Death walked in unannounced, and begged the gentleman to come along as quickly as possible, as there were a good many more people to be called for that afternoon.

"But I can't," cried the gentleman, in dismay. "I really can't, you know. I—why, I've asked some people to dine with me this evening."

"That's a little too much," said Death. And the devil carried the gentleman off in a big black bag.

X.

There was once a man who had seen the Parthenon, and he wished to build his god a temple like it.

But he was not a skillful man, and, try as be would, he could produce only a mud hut thatched with straw; and he sat down and wept because he could not build a temple for his god.

But one who passed by said to him:

"There are two worse plights than yours. One is to have no god; the other is to build a mud hut and mistake it for the Parthenon."

Florence Merriam [1863–1948][32]

from Birds through an Opera Glass

Catbird

High trees have an unsocial aspect, and so, as Lowell says, "The catbird croons in the lilac-bush," in the alders, in a prickly ash copse, a barberry-bush, or by the side of the garden. In Northampton one of his favorite haunts is an old orchard that slopes down to the edge of Mill River. Here he is welcomed every year by his college girl friends; and in the open seclusion of an apple-tree proceeds to build his nest and raise his little family, singing through it all with keen enjoyment of the warm sunshine and his own company.

To the tyro the catbird is at once the most interesting and most exasperating of birds. Like some people, he seems to give up his time to the pleasure of hearing himself talk. A first cousin of the mocking-bird—whom he resembles in person much more than in voice—perhaps the relationship accounts for his overweening confidence in his vocal powers. As a matter of fact his jerky utterance is so harsh that it has been aptly termed asthmatic.

The catbird is unmistakably a Bohemian. He is exquisitely formed, and has a beautiful slate-gray coat, set off by his black head and tail. By nature he is peculiarly graceful, and when he chooses can pass for the most polished of the Philistine aristocracy. But he cares nothing for all this. With lazy self-indulgence he sits by the hour with relaxed muscles, and listlessly drooping wings and tail. If he were a man you feel confident that he would sit in shirt sleeves at home and go on the street without a collar.

And his occupation? His cousin is an artist, but he—is he a wag as well as a caricaturist, or is he in sober earnest when he tries to mimic the inimitable Wilson's thrush? If a wag he is a success, for he deceives the unguarded into believing him a robin, a cat, and—"a bird new to science!" How he must chuckle over the enthusiasm which hails his various notes and the bewilderment and chagrin that come to the diligent observer who finally catches a glimpse of the garrulous mimic!

The catbird builds his nest as he does everything else. The loose mass of coarse twigs patched up with pieces of newspaper or anything he happens to fancy, looks as if it would hardly bear his weight. He lines it, however, with fine bits of brown and black roots, and when the beautiful dark green eggs are laid in it, you feel sure that such an artistic looking bird must enjoy the contrasting colors.

Snow Bunting; Snowflake

This is the true snowbird, and though it belongs in the same pigeon-hole—that of the finches and sparrows—it can never be confounded with the junco. The monastic juncos are closely shrouded in slate-gray robes and cowls, only a short under robe of white being marked off below their breasts. The snowflakes, on the other hand, as their name suggests, are mostly white, although their backs are streaked with dusky and black.

The juncos come about the house in spring and fall, and during the early snows, but the snowbirds, timid and strange, fly over the fields and are associated with the wonderful white days of a country winter, when the sky is white, the earth is white, and the white trees bow silently under the wand of winter till they stand an enchanted snow forest. For, as the flakes drift through the air, the snowbirds, undulating between the white earth and sky, seem like wandering spirits that are a part of the all-pervading whiteness. Thoreau says, "they are the true spirits of the snowstorm. They are the animated beings that ride upon it and have their life in it."

Mr. Allen, in speaking of our winter birds, says "The beautiful snow buntings when whirling from field to field in compact flocks, their white wings glistening in the sunlight, form one of the most attractive sights of winter." He adds that they are the "bad weather birds" of the superstitious, as they usually appear mysteriously during snowstorms and disappear in the weeks of fine weather. He says: "Cold, half-arctic countries being their chosen home, they only favor us with their presence during those short intervals when their food in the northern fields is too deeply buried; and being strong of wing and exceedingly rapid in flight, they can in a few hours leave the plain for the mountain, or migrate hundreds of miles to the northward."

Late in December I have seen a flock of them flying over the meadows with the rhythmical undulating motion of their cousins the goldfinches, twittering *ter-ra-lee, ter-ra-lee, ter-ra-lee* as they went. Now and then they would light for a moment to pick at the seeds appearing above the snow, but soon they swept on toward the north.

Robert W. Chambers [1865–1933][33]

from THE PROPHETS' PARADISE

THE STUDIO

He smiled, saying, "Seek her throughout the world."

I said: "Why tell me of the world? My world is here, between these walls and the sheet of glass above; here among gilded flagons and dull jeweled arms, tarnished frames and canvases, black chests and high-backed chairs, quaintly carved and stained in blue and gold."

"For whom do you wait?" he said, and I answered, "When she comes I shall know her."

On my hearth a tongue of flame whispered secrets to the whitening ashes. In the street below I heard footsteps, a voice, and a song.

"For whom, then, do you wait?" he said, and I answered, "I shall know her."

Footsteps, a voice, and a song in the street below, and I knew the song, but neither the steps nor the voice.

"Fool!" he cried, "the song is the same, the voice and steps have but changed with years!"

On the hearth a tongue of flame whispered above the whitening ashes: "Wait no more; they have passed—the steps and the voice in the street below."

Then he smiled, saying, "For whom do you wait? Seek her throughout the world!"

I answered: "My world is here between these walls and the sheet of glass above; here among gilded flagons and dull jeweled arms, tarnished frames and canvases, black chests and high-backed chairs, quaintly carved and stained in blue and gold."

THE SACRIFICE

I went into a field of flowers, whose petals are whiter than snow and whose hearts are pure gold.

Far afield a woman cried, "I have killed him I loved!" and from a jar she poured blood upon the flowers whose petals are whiter than snow and whose hearts are pure gold.

Far afield I followed, and on the jar I read a thousand names, while from within the fresh blood bubbled to the brim.

"I have killed him I loved!" she cried. "The world's athirst; now let it drink!" She passed, and far afield I watched her pouring blood upon the flowers whose petals are whiter than snow and whose hearts are pure gold.

The Throng

There, where the throng was thickest in the street, I stood with Pierrot. All eyes were turned on me.

"What are they laughing at?" I asked; but he grinned, dusting the chalk from my black cloak. "I cannot see; it must be something droll, perhaps an honest thief!"

All eyes were turned on me.

"He has robbed you of your purse!" they laughed.

"My purse!" I cried; "Pierrot—help! It is a thief!"

They laughed: "He has robbed you of your purse!"

Then Truth stepped out, holding a mirror. "If he is an honest thief," cried Truth, "Pierrot shall find him with this mirror!" But he only grinned, dusting the chalk from my black cloak.

"You see," he said, "Truth is an honest thief; she brings you back your mirror."

All eyes were turned on me.

"Arrest Truth!" I cried, forgetting it was not a mirror but a purse I lost, standing with Pierrot, there, where the throng was thickest in the street.

The Green-Room

The Clown turned his powdered face to the mirror.

"If to be fair is to be beautiful," he said, "who can compare with me in my white mask?"

"Who can compare with him in his white mask?" I asked of Death beside me.

"Who can compare with me?" said Death, "for I am paler still."

"You are very beautiful," sighed the Clown, turning his powdered face from the mirror.

Bruce Porter [1865–1953][34]

The Return of Spring

Now the iris is in bloom, and I lie between the rattling spears and under the banners, purple and gold, of an invading army, marching up the slopes from the sea.

What an infinity of silent life in these green vistas of the grass!—camp followers and foragers—burnished beetles and lady-birds—hurtling ants and tremulous blind lice, their translucent bodies filled with green fire! Strange shadowed world! What combats—what matings! And then, what catastrophes of obliterated lives and passions following my footfall!

But above me, a tumult of clamoring acclamation! Hear the wind, and all the voices of the sea, and the trilling of larks and linnets, and the creeling of the gulls! A rich and good earth—this: breathing incense of fresh growth to the Sun, her lord.

Naked and at ease in the world, with the sun warm on your shoulders and the grass cool against your side—here is a cheap delight—unknown to kings in their pleasures.

To keep a quick heart for your fellows—to fear neither God nor man—nor your own soul!—to worship beauty, and to love truth—Ah! with this blossom of the iris, I give you the key of life!

But I, alas! have not yet found the door.

Gelett Burgess [1866–1951][35]

The Adjective Family

It is the Adjective family, to be sure, that has caused most disturbance in the domain of Rhetoric. They are of a meddlesome sort when not kept under strict vision—all very well in their way, but, like spoiled children, over fond of protrudence. Yet the Substantives hanker after them as for borrowed finery, and cock themselves in their meaningless adornment till you can scarce tell them apart. A few only, like *gentlemen,* will have none of the brood, and dare go unattended like Don Caesar de Bazan. But it is for the most part an internecine strife among the adjectives—the quarrels of the servants below stairs, that season the scandals of verbiage; and of all the brotherhood, intolerable and inconsequent, are the brats *very* and *quite,* both widely astray from the strict duties to which they were bred, and in their second childhood of dotage. The one was used to do good service to the noun, but now dandles at the heels of his lustier kinsmen, useless as the wings on an ostrich, a mere degenerate appendage. The other's career is still more fatuous. Its evil companionship corrupts the manners of decent adjectives, whose value he borrows to squander on mere sound. I wonder that such staid words as *remarkable* and *characteristic* will support such parasites. *Unique, exceptional* and *extreme,* once dignified beyond comparison, are past all hope, and have been flattered into a pitiful declension.

Even *every,* straight-laced little modifier, has got to aping the disbehavior, and tags such phrases as *now and then* with his vulgar attachment, as yokels wont to ridicule their mates on All Fools' Day. Almost excusable are the few that fail in the honest endeavor to carry their meanings safely, though they are delivered at the wrong places. *Only* is the most stupid of these, and is notorious by his blunders, always turning up at the wrong end of the sentence. *Healthy* is also the type of many well-meaning adjectives that are fond of attempting to do the work of similar-sounding brothers, while others, like *condign,* fly wider of the mark and are forever charging into others' business, adding fatal confusion to the phrase.

Some adjectives disport themselves as adverbs, like women trying to be men. The verb *to look* has led many of them astray, but *like* is the very Mrs. Bloomer of their set, all but unsexed by misuse.

But there is a still more wanton crew with all significance dissipated by abandon, their proud names smirched and their manners debased by vicious indulgence. Such are *awful, elegant,* and the rest, now common as the Paris road; and *nice* and *pretty* will be with them soon also, if they remain as spendthrift.

Many of our adjectives, immigrant to the New World of Letters, have renounced allegiance to the old forms, and are now naturalized citizens, adopting the customs of their environs. *Smart & Cunning* are already fairly well-to-do and respectable in their American establishment, and have almost forgotten their British antecedents.

And knocking patiently at the door of respectability is a horde of unregenerate upstarts—tatterdemalion and fantastic importations from the world of Slang. Some enter and recruit the language with vigorous and adjuvant blood, but most are here to-day and off to-morrow, coming out of Nowhere, and tramping it back to the same foreign seaport.

But aloof even from such shabby gentility as has been remarked—dwellers in the very purlieus of Rhetoric, hang a caste prescribed; unmentioned by lips polite, walkers of the street since Shakespeare's time—the devil's superlatives. But the new *régime* has come, oaths have lost their meaning in the dawn of reason, old shackles are unsprung, and the d—— may come by his rights at last!

The Mutual Advice Association

What poet would not know the truthful tenor of the public mind—the free untrammeled judgment of the ones who read, not those who write? What artist would not care for frank and honest criticism of his brother men, instead of prying in the cynic pages of the paid-for press? What simple, plain and modest citizen but longs to know what voices speak behind him as he passes on the street, what figure in the public eye he cuts; and what ambitious youth but wonders to himself the color of his praise and blame, the true effect of words and dress? What debutante in launching forth her lovely craft on social seas but feels the looks she cannot read, and in the buzz of whispers hears her name, all ignorant of the adjectives applied? What new-betrothed that introduces to his smiling friends the maiden of his choice but fears to guess what lies beneath the gilded words; her social standing set, her face and talents nicely gauged, and he of all

deceived and ignorant?
Subscribe to the Lark's

❧ ❧ Mutual Advice Association ❧ ❧

Confidential agents in every large city will investigate any desired phase of your life, converse frankly and fully with your friends, and report at length with anonymous quotations. Voluntary opinions carefully collected and classified. Favorable comments reported to those desiring encouragement, and harsher criticisms to those of morbid conscience. Both kinds forwarded if desired. Clipping Bureaus and Commercial Agencies are but partially discriminating evidences. *Get the whole truth.* All communications mailed in plain sealed envelope.

Terms, $5.00 for 100 quotations, payable in advance. Address, stating character of investigation desired, to The Lark's Mutual Advice Association, San Francisco.

The Confessions of a Yellster

I was boisterous and turbulent as a youth, a loud mouthed, impossible sort of a boy;—one to be kept out of doors as long as possible, and to be suppressed at night by every means in a mother's power. I was sent to boarding school, but was speedily expelled for my noise. I managed to get into college at last, and there I was perfectly happy, rooting on the campus and on the football field at all hours, with the more enthusiastic of my mates. Where there was a yell, there was I, the king-pin of the hullabaloo; a shouting mania possessed me, and I was the leader in all the celebrations of the University. I invented new cries and captained that vocal patriotism by which classes triumph, and battles are supposed to be won upon the gridiron. I had a large chest-expansion, and was known far and wide as a man of mighty lungs.

After I was graduated, I obtained a clerkship in a wholesale-house, and attempted to gain a mastery over my madness, but the effort was terrible. After every day of silence, I sought the unfrequented suburban districts, and screamed to the moon and all the planets, to relieve the tension of my desire. How I envied the retail-counter clerks, who were privileged to vociferate "Cash!" till the windows rattled! I often woke myself, and all the neighbors, by my midnight shrieks, breaking through dreams, happy dreams, where I trumpeted at fires or on ship-board, whooped with wild Apaches, or bawled with frenzied negroid Voodoos.

So things went from bad to worse. I dared not trust myself in society, lest I should explode with my pent-up feelings, and breed a scandal among my respectable friends. But at last the climax came, on a Sunday when I made a final attempt to calm myself in the odor of sanctity at a neighbouring church. The dim light of the edifice and the peaceful serenity of the congregation sobered me when I entered, and I thanked God that I was, for once, like other men. When I had begun to tire of the stillness, the harsh blare of the organ and the raucous notes of the tenor soothed me again; I delighted in the discords, for it was an ill-paid choir, and I settled myself in content. But alas, I had not calculated upon the agony of that Rector's voice! His first low and solemn words began the torture, and at each succeeding droning sentence, the barb of annoyance sunk deeper into my spirit. I itched all over, with the monotony of his whining modulations. I held up first one foot, and then the other, to distract my mind from the drawling moan of the voice; I counted the windows and the nodding heads of the worshippers; I began to wonder what would happen if I should give way under the strain, and the temptation grew suddenly like a cyclone, blowing down every barrier of decency. I held my breath in terror of the demon that possessed me, while the congregation swayed before my eyes in a dull blur. Still the Rector's voice murmured unceasingly, and like an earache that grows more and more intense, at last my desire boiled up and overflowed my soul. I rose to my feet and yelled aloud! One mad, hoarse shriek, that echoed back from the chancel, raced up and down the aisles, leaped to the vaulted roof, and swept down upon the drowsy audience. An hundred heads swung round to me, an hundred white faces confronted me with staring eyes. The Preacher stopped suddenly; there was a crescendo of astonished exclamations; a woman screamed, two grey-bearded deacons hurried toward me, and I reeled into the arms of a verger.

• • •

I am happy now, thanks to the wise services of the physician that attended me; and all day long I have the blessed right to yell "*Fresh Mack-er-el!*" upon the highways and byways of the town. No one stares at me as I pass, scream loudly as I may; and at night, after a day of indescribable ecstasy, I retire to my little garden and practice upon my trombone. And when I go to sleep, my dreams are full of peace.

Ernest Dowson [1867–1900][36]

from DECORATIONS IN PROSE

ABSINTHIA TAETRA

Green changed to white, emerald to an opal: nothing was changed.

The man let the water trickle gently into his glass, and as the green clouded, a mist fell away from his mind.

Then he drank opaline.

Memories and terrors beset him. The past tore after him like a panther and through the blackness of the present he saw the luminous tiger eyes of the things to be.

But he drank opaline.

And that obscure night of the soul, and the valley of humiliation, through which he stumbled were forgotten. He saw blue vistas of undiscovered countries, high prospects and a quiet, caressing sea. The past shed its perfume over him, to-day held his hand as it were a little child, and to-morrow shone like a white star: nothing was changed.

He drank opaline.

The man had known the obscure night of the soul, and lay even now in the valley of humiliation; and the tiger menace of the things to be was red in the skies. But for a little while he had forgotten.

Green changed to white, emerald to an opal: nothing was changed.

THE VISIT

As though I were still struggling through the meshes of some riotous dream, I heard his knock upon the door. As in a dream, I bade him enter, but with his entry, I awoke. Yet when he entered it seemed to me that I was dreaming, for there was nothing strange in that supreme and sorrowful smile which shone through the mask which I knew. And just as though I had not always been afraid of him I said: "Welcome."

And he said very simply, "I am here."

Dreaming I had thought myself, but the reproachful sorrow of his smile showed me that I was awake. Then dared I open my eyes and I saw my old body on the bed, and the room in which I had grown so tired, and in the middle of the room the pan of charcoal which still smouldered. And dimly I remembered my great weariness and the lost whiteness of Lalage and last year's snows; and these things had been agonies.

Darkly, as in a dream, I wondered why they gave me no more hurt, as I looked at my old body on the bed; why, they were like old maids' fancies (as I looked at my gray body on the bed of my agonies)—like silly toys of children that fond mothers lay up in lavender (as I looked at the twisted limbs of my old body), for these things had been agonies.

But all my wonder was gone when I looked again into the eyes of my guest, and I said:

"I have wanted you all my life."

Then said Death (and what reproachful tenderness was shadowed in his obscure smile):

"You had only to call."

The Princess of Dreams

Poor legendary Princess! In her enchaunted tower of ivory, the liberator thought that she awaited him.

For once in a dream he had seen, as they were flowers de luce, the blue lakes of her eyes had seemed to be enveloped in a tangle of her golden hair.

And he sought her through the countless windings of her forest for many moons, sought her through the morasses, sparing not his horse nor his sword. On his way he slew certain evil magicians and many of his friends, so that at his journey's end his bright sword was tarnished and his comeliness swart with mud. His horses he had not spared: their bones made a white track behind him in the windings of the forest: but he still bore her ransom, all the costly, graceful things stored in a cypress chest: massed pearls and amethysts and silks from Samarcand, Valance of Venice, and fine tapestry of Tyre. All these he brought with him to the gates of her ivory tower.

Poor legendary princess.

For he did not free her and the fustian porter took his treasure and broke his stained sword in two.

And who knows where he went, horseless and disarmed, through the morasses and the dark windings of her forest under the moonless night, dreaming of those blue lakes which were flowers de luce, her eyes? Who knows? For the fustian porter says nothing, being slow of wit.

But there are some who say that she had no wish to be freed, and that those flowers de luce, her eyes, are a stagnant, dark pool, that her glorious golden hair was only long enough to reach her postern gate.

Some say, moreover, that her tower is not of ivory and that she is not even virtuous nor a princess.

Stephen Crane [1871-1900][37]

The Judgment of the Sage

A beggar crept wailing through the streets of a city. A certain man came to him there and gave him bread, saying: "I give you this loaf, because of God's word." Another came to the beggar and gave him bread, saying: "Take this loaf; I give it because you are hungry."

Now there was a continual rivalry among the citizens of this town as to who should appear to be the most pious man, and the event of the gifts to the beggar made discussion. People gathered in knots and argued furiously to no particular purpose. They appealed to the beggar, but he bowed humbly to the ground, as befitted one of his condition, and answered: "It is a singular circumstance that the loaves were of one size and of the same quality. How, then, can I decide which of these men gave bread more piously?"

The people heard of a philosopher who travelled through their country, and one said: "Behold, we who give not bread to beggars are not capable of judging those who have given bread to beggars. Let us, then, consult this wise man."

"But," said some, "mayhap this philosopher, according to your rule that one must have given bread before judging they who give bread, will not be capable."

"That is an indifferent matter to all truly great philosophers." So they made search for the wise man, and in time they came upon him, strolling along at his ease in the manner of philosophers.

"Oh, most illustrious sage," they cried.

"Yes," said the philosopher promptly.

"Oh, most illustrious sage, there are two men in our city, and one gave bread to a beggar, saying: 'Because of God's word.' And the other gave bread to the beggar, saying: 'Because you are hungry.' Now, which of these, oh, most illustrious sage, is the more pious man?"

"Eh?" said the philosopher.

"Which of these, oh, most illustrious sage, is the more pious man?"

"My friends," said the philosopher suavely addressing the concourse, "I see that you mistake me for an illustrious sage. I am not he whom you seek.

However, I saw a man answering my description pass here some time ago. With speed you may overtake him. Adieu."

The Seaside Hotel Hop

The seaside hotel hop is an institution peculiar unto itself. It is generally held on Saturday evening when a few extra dancing men come down in the pursuit of Sunday rest (?). There are usually from 200 to 600 people looking on, and occasionally as many as six couples on the floor, though this highwater mark is not often reached. The music varies with the character of the hotel, but is likely to consist of a wailing cornet and a piano, which resemble a Christian who hath not charity, in that it long ago became as sounding brass and tinkling cymbal. The music plays right along by the hour whether anybody is dancing or not. Occasionally the hotel proprietor looks in, rubbing his hands and beaming on the scene with an air that says, "Enjoy yourselves, my people, these riotous festivities are given away with every package of twenty meal tickets."

Early in the evening the floor is taken up by skinny little girls with curls, short white dresses and a superabundance of blue ribbon, who perform "dancing in the barn" and other gems of the dancing-school, to the delight of admiring parents. After an army of nurses have cleared the floor of the small fry, the sun-browned summer girl comes in from her retreat around on the dark side of the veranda. Her ball dress is evidently cut lower in the neck than her bathing suit, which makes her look like a doll with a bronze head on a porcelain body. She dances somewhat recklessly as one who is aware that the eyes of seventeen ancient and honorable spinsters in the front row are upon her, and has determined to show her contempt for, and independence of, "the horrid old things." Her partner is a young man with tender, yearning eyes, a struggling mustache, a tennis shirt and russet shoes. He holds her—well, as if he were afraid of losing her.

When a set is made up for the lancers it is composed of people from seven different States. As the figures for the lancers are never danced alike in any two localities, and there is no prompter, a general tangle results. "Brother Tom, from college," creates an additional ruction by pressing all the girls' hands in the "grand right and left," and swinging them off their feet at "balance the corners." A number of men in evening dress wander wearily about and do the "heavy standing around" but never dance. Only the men in tennis shirts dance.

In the hotel dining-room or parlor where the hop is going on it is as hot as a furnace. The windows are blocked up with people who are too old or too weary of life to dance, and with visitors from the neighboring boarding-houses which have not risen to the dignity of a hop. In a secluded corner of the veranda the coterie of dashing widows and young married women have ensconced themselves with their following of mature admirers. Throughout the evening they dispose of endless lemonades containing a certain percentage of woody fiber commonly called "stick."

At ten minutes to 12 o'clock the cornet wails its last wail and the piano thumps its last thump. The bronzed maidens of the dance drag themselves up stairs jingling their room-keys and dropping an occasional joke for the benefit of the night clerk. The men smoke their good-night cigars on the veranda while they cool off and listen to the booming breakers on the shore. A Sunday quiet settles down over the frail fabric of a summer hotel, unless the forty-seven babies wake up and howl their midnight chorus, or the fat man with the thirty-two foot diapason snore gets "cast" on his back and rouses the furthermost echoes of the whispering gallery into which 500 people are packed.

How the Donkey Lifted the Hills

Many people suppose that the donkey is lazy. This is a great mistake. It is his pride.

Years ago, there was nobody quite so fine as the donkey. He was a great swell in those times. No one could express an opinion of anything without the donkey showing him where he was wrong in it. No one could mention the name of an important personage without the donkey declaring how well he knew him.

The donkey was above all things a proud and aristocratic beast.

One day a party of animals were discussing one thing and another, until finally the conversation drifted around to mythology.

"I have always admired that giant, Atlas," observed the ox in the course of the conversation. "It was amazing how he could carry things."

"Oh, yes, Atlas," said the donkey. "I knew him very well. I once met a man and we got talking of Atlas. I expressed my admiration for the giant and my desire to meet him some day, if possible. Whereupon the man said that there was nothing quite so easy. He was sure that his dear friend, Atlas, would be happy to meet so charming a donkey. Was I at leisure next Monday? Well, then, could I dine with him upon that date? So, you see, it was all arranged. I found Atlas to be a very pleasant fellow."

"It has always been a wonder to me how he could have carried the earth on his back," said the horse.

"Oh, my dear sir, nothing is more simple," cried the donkey. "One has only to make up one's mind to it and then—do it. That is all. I am quite sure that if I wished I could carry a range of mountains upon my back."

All the others said, "Oh, my!"

"Yes I could," asserted the donkey, stoutly. "It is merely a question of making up one's mind. I will bet."

"I will wager also," said the horse. "I will wager my ears that you can't carry a range of mountains upon your back."

"Done," cried the donkey.

Forthwith the party of animals set out for the mountains. Suddenly, however, the donkey paused and said: "Oh, but look here! Who will place this range of mountains upon my back? Surely I cannot be expected to do the loading also."

Here was a great question. The party consulted. At length the ox said: "We will have to ask some men to shovel the mountains upon the donkey's back."

Most of the others clapped their hoofs or their paws and cried: "Ah, that is the thing."

The horse, however, shook his head doubtfully. "I don't know about these men. They are very sly. They will introduce some deviltry into the affair."

"Why, how silly," said the donkey. "Apparently you do not understand men. They are the most gentle, guileless creatures."

"Well," retorted the horse, "I will doubtless be able to escape since I am not to be encumbered with any mountains. Proceed."

The donkey smiled in derision at these observations by the horse.

Presently they came upon some men who were laboring away like mad, digging ditches, felling trees, gathering fruits, carrying water, building huts.

"Look at these men, would you," said the horse. "Can you trust them after this exhibition of their depravity? See how each one selfishly——"

The donkey interrupted with a loud laugh.

"What nonsense!"

And then he cried out to the men: "Ho, my friends, will you please come and shovel a range of mountains upon my back?"

"What?"

"Will you please come and shovel a range of mountains upon my back?"

The men were silent for a time. Then they went apart and debated. They gesticulated a great deal.

Some apparently said one thing and some another. At last they paused and one of their number came forward.

"Why do you wish a range of mountains shoveled upon your back?"

"It is a wager," cried the donkey.

The men consulted again. And, as the discussion became older, their heads went closer and closer together, until they merely whispered, and did not gesticulate at all. Ultimately they cried: "Yes, certainly we will shovel a range of mountains upon your back for you."

"Ah, thanks," said the donkey.

"Here is surely some deviltry," said the horse behind his hoof to the ox. The entire party proceeded then to the mountains. The donkey drew a long breath and braced his legs.

"Are you ready?" asked the men.

"All ready," cried the donkey.

The men began to shovel.

The dirt and the stones flew over the donkey's back in showers. It was not long before his legs were hidden. Presently only his neck and head remained in view. Then at last this wise donkey vanished. There had been made no great effect upon the range of mountains. They still towered toward the sky.

The watching crowd saw the heap of dirt and stones make a little movement and then was heard a muffled cry. "Enough! Enough! It was not two ranges of mountains. The wager was for one range of mountains. It is not fair! It is not fair!"

But the new men only laughed as they shoveled on.

"Enough! Enough! Oh, woe is me—thirty snow-capped peaks upon my little back. Ah, these false, false men. Oh, virtuous, wise and holy men, desist."

The men again laughed. They were as busy as fiends with their shovels.

"Ah, brutal, cowardly, accursed men, ah, good, gentle and holy men, please remove some of those damnable peaks. I will adore your beautiful shovels forever. I will be a slave to the beckoning of your little fingers. I will no longer be my own donkey—I will be your donkey."

The men burst into a triumphant shout and ceased shoveling.

"Swear it, mountain-carrier!"

"I swear! I swear! I swear!"

The other animals scampered away then, for these men in their plots and plans were very terrible. "Poor old foolish fellow," cried the horse; "he may keep his ears. He will need them to hear and count the blows that are now to fall upon him."

The men unearthed the donkey. They beat him with their shovels. "Ho, come on, slave." Encrusted with earth, yellow-eyed from fright, the donkey limped towards his prison. His ears hung down like the leaves of the plantain during the great rain.

So now, when you see a donkey with a church, a palace, and three villages upon his back, and he goes with infinite slowness, moving but one leg at a time, do not think him lazy. It is his pride.

John Millington Synge [1871–1909][38]

from Translations from Petrarch: Sonnets from "Laura in Death"

He Wishes He Might Die and Follow Laura

In the years of her age the most beautiful and the most flowery—the time Love has his mastery—Laura, who was my life, has gone away leaving the earth stripped and desolate. She has gone up into the Heavens, living and beautiful and naked, and from that place she is keeping her Lordship and her rein upon me, and I crying out: Ohone, when will I see that day breaking that will be my first day with herself in Paradise?

My thoughts are going after her, and it is that way my soul would follow her, lightly, and airily, and happily, and I would be rid of all my great troubles. But what is delaying me is the proper thing to lose me utterly, to make me a greater weight on my own self.

Oh, what a sweet death I might have died this day three years to-day!

Laura is Ever Present to Him

If the birds are making lamentation, or the green banks are moved by a little wind of summer, or you can hear the waters making a stir by the shores that are green and flowery.

That's where I do be stretched out thinking of love, writing my songs, and herself that Heaven shows me though hidden in the earth I set my eyes on, and hear the way that she feels my sighs and makes an answer to me.

"Alas," I hear her say, "why are you using yourself up before the time is come, and pouring out a stream of tears so sad and doleful.

"You'd do right to be glad rather, for in dying I won days that have no ending, and when you saw me shutting up my eyes I was opening them on the light that is eternal."

The Fine Time of the Year Increases Petrarch's Sorrow

The south wind is coming back, bringing the fine season, and the flowers, and the grass, her sweet family, along with her. The swallow and the nightingale are making a stir, and the spring is turning white and red in every place.

There is a cheerful look on the meadows, and peace in the sky, and the sun is well pleased, I'm thinking, looking downward, and the air and the waters and the earth herself are full of love, and every beast is turning back looking for its mate.

And what is coming to me is great sighing and trouble, which herself is drawing out of my deep heart, herself that has taken the key of it up to Heaven.

And it is this way I am, that the singing birds, and the flowers of the earth, and the sweet ladies, with their grace and comeliness, are the like of a desert to me, and wild beasts astray in it.

Laura Waits for Him in Heaven

The first day she passed up and down through the Heavens, gentle and simple were left standing, and they in great wonder, saying one to the other:

"What new light is that? What new beauty at all? The like of herself hasn't risen up these long years from the common world."

And herself, well pleased with the Heavens, was going forward, matching herself with the most perfect that were before her, yet one time, and another, waiting a little, and turning her head back to see if myself was coming after her. It's for that I'm lifting up all my thoughts and will into the Heavens, because I do hear her praying that I should be making haste for ever.

Harrison G. Rhodes [1871-1929][39]

Sketches

I have been copying an essay steadily all the evening. My head aches, my fingers are wearied, and as I stare with blinking eyes at the glaring white paper, the letters I have scrawled on it dance in the brilliant lamp-light like demons. I close my eyes and I put my hand to my head in utter exhaustion. After a minute I open my eyes and say to myself,

"I will finish this page and then stop."

I go on.

. . . The prologue began with these peculiarly Johnsonian lines,

"Pressed by the load of life the weary mind
Surveys the general toil of humankind." . . .

It is too much. I throw down my pen with fierce despair. It lands on the point and stands erect on the blotting paper which covers the desk. I get up. The rain is pouring monotonously down; my fire is flickering out; I can hear my chum snoring in his bed; the clock strikes two.

"General toil of humankind. Nonsense! As if any fool but myself were working at this time."

I go to the window. Across the street, in a glare of light in one of the windows, I see two Chinamen ironing shirts.

* * *

In the days when Brigham Young was directing the theocratic government of Utah, the Mormon missionaries in England converted a one-legged man near Dulwich. This man, now strong in faith, conceived the idea that the prophet in Salt Lake City might effect a miraculous restoration of the leg which he had lost in an accident. So a month later he presented himself, weary and travel-stained, but full of cheerful hope, before the head of the Mormon church, and told his desires. Strange as it may seem, the prophet said he would willingly get him a new leg; but begged him first to consider the matter fully. This life, he told him, is but a vale of tears and as nothing compared to eternity. He was making the choice of going through life with one leg and having two after the resurrection, or of having two legs through life and three after. The man found the prospect of being a human tripod through all eternity so uncongenial that he accepted with resignation his present lot and excused the prophet from performing the miracle.

* * *

The chancel screen is twined with evergreen and bound with holly. Through its dark bars, the white reredos gleams with its candles, brighter than ever, as if seen in the blaze of sunlight through twining vines and undergrowth from out the darkness of the woods. Against the whiteness on the altar table shines the vivid scarlet of the flowers in the vases. Before the altar kneel the acolytes in their red gowns: on either side, the choir boys in black and white. Above their heads hang the brass lamps with their little crimson flames: the middle one, hanging lowest, sways gently to and fro, as if keeping time to the monotonous intonations of the priest's chant. I watch its swinging, and as thoughts wander I follow its little light till I blink and my eyes fill with tears. Then I look away to the carved heads on the pillars above the organ and down again to the white-haired organist. As I watch him, the organ sends out a soft thread of melody which ripples down from the faint high notes of the treble—like the music of the descent of the Holy Graèl in "Lohengrin." I slip mechanically back into my seat: the prayer is ended.

Dora Greenwell McChesney [1871–1912][40]

At Old Italian Casements

From a Tuscan Window

A high dark Florentine palace with frowning cornice and barred windows, rich torch-holders of wrought iron set beside the deep-arched doorway. In one of the casements stands a young girl; it is early morning and the fresh light shines over her. She has been, perhaps, at a banquet, for she is in gala dress—soft green worked with threads of silver; about her slim long throat is a chain with an ornament of enamel bright with shifting colours. She grasps the heavy iron with a small white hand and leans forward; the shadow of one bar lies like a dark band across the bright hair drawn smoothly back from her forehead. She is watching for her lover to pass in the dusky street; her lips are grave, but there is a smile in the brown eyes under the fine curved brows. She looks out through the sunrise and waits. Underneath the window, so close to the wall that he cannot be seen from above, lies a youth wrapped in a dark mantle—dead—he has been stabbed there in the night and fallen quite silently. His loose dark hair brushes the ground where he lies; his blood has made a stain on the grey stones. His white face is turned up; his eyes arc open, looking towards the casement—the casement where the maiden leans, watching for her lover to pass in the sunrise.

In the Palace of the Duke

The window is wreathed about with strange carvings, where mocking faces look from among the vines. Against the broad sill a youth is leaning, looking into the court below where his horse is being led out and his falconer is waiting. The lad is dressed with great richness, his close crimson doublet and hosen curiously slashed and his short cloak thick with golden embroidery. His dark hair makes a cloud about a delicate willful face. In one hand he holds a casket of amber wrought with the loves of the gods, and before him on the ledge lie papers newly signed. Close by him are two figures; a man still young and a stately woman whose hair is grey beneath her jewelled head-dress and veil. They are mother and son, for their features are alike, and wasted alike before the time by some long hunger of desire. She has her left hand on her bosom, pressed hard almost as though on something hidden there; with her right she holds a goblet of silver to the youth, who reaches backwards for it, not turning, with an indolent gesture. He glances carelessly to the court below, but the eyes of mother and son have met, unflinchingly, in a slow smile of terrible understanding.

A Venetian Balcony

Night on the waters, yet no darkness. On the still lagoons broad sheen of moonlight; in the canals and squares of Venice shifting and dashing lights of many lamps and torches, for it is a night of festival. From a balcony set with discs of alabaster, purple and white, a woman is bending to look across the water. She is full in the mingling of lights, white of the moon-beams, gold of the wide-flaring torches; they shine on the warm whiteness of brow and throat and bosom and the gold of her hair which she wears coiled high, like a crown, about a jewelled dagger. She holds her mask in her left hand on which is no ring. There is a smile on her proud lips, but the great fire of her eyes is dying; into the triumph is stealing a touch of fear and the sense of a woman's first surrender. The night is all but gone, the revelry at its close. She looks across the water where the moon has made a silver track, but her eyes seek only the track of a gondola which has passed—slipped from her sight. Back in the dusk rich room a single silver lamp is burning; it throws a gleam on her own picture. A master hand has set her there as the holy Saint Catherine, robed like a queen, as indeed she is this night, but kneeling humbly before the Blessed Babe and holding a spousal ring.

A Brother of St. Francis

Low and narrow, the window of a convent cell, but it commands the width of Umbrian plain, above which the sun is scarcely risen. A great band of saffron light outlines the far horizon, but the full day has not come. Close to the walls of the cloister rise slender trees, shooting up as if athirst for the sun, their tall stems bare and straight, only breaking at the top into leafage.

These lift a delicate tracery of green against the rose-grey of the sky, but, beyond, the lower slopes are dim with the ashen mist of the olives. And still beyond the plain sweeps out, showing no wood or stream, making ready wide barren spaces to be touched into beauty by the changing sky. The sun has hardly given full life to the colours beneath; the green and yellow and grey merge tremulously. The virginal air of early dawn is not yet brushed away. The plain lies dream-like—rapt in a great expectancy. From the casement a young monk looks out. He wears the brown habit of a Franciscan. His eyes are wide and fixed and he looks into the sunrise and beyond it. His face is worn and very pale, so that the early light seems to shine through it, meeting a light from within; his lips are parted, not in prayer but in some breathless rapture of contemplation. The morning brightness searches his barren cell, touches his coarse garments and his clasped hands. The marks of fast and vigil are upon him. In his face is the fullness of utter renunciation—and the peace of a great promise. Outside, above the narrow window of his cell, the mated birds are building.

The Cardinal's Outlook

Wide splendor of the sunset beating down upon Rome; the statues on column and church front stand aloof, and uplifted in the red glow the dark shafts of the cypresses are kindled by it into dusky gold. It shines in at the window where the Cardinal is sitting and dwells on his rich robes—then is subdued and lost in the room behind. Yet even there fugitive gleams respond to it, from rare enamel and wrought metal; most of all from the statuette of a Bacchante, the golden bronze of which seems to hold the sun-rays. The ivory crucifix looks wan beside it. The Cardinal does not see the sunset, though a bar of brightness lies across the book open before him on which his left hand is pressed. The window is not all in light; outside, against the pageant of the sky rises a mighty bulk of darkness. It is the dome of St. Peter's. Its shadow lies across the Cardinal's dwelling and across the world of his thought. And there—close to the base of that dome, there in the heart of the Vatican, the Pope is dying. The Cardinal, new come from his bedside, sits waiting: soon the last mystic sacraments must be bestowed, soon the last throb of life must pass. He waits. He does not see the sunset; he sees instead the kneeling forms round the death-bed; he sees the shrouded halls and solemn gatherings of the Conclave. He sees—beyond—a mystery of ever widening domination, at the centre of which is enthroned—not the old man who is dying yonder. Whose will it be—the solitary sovereign figure, soon to stand there where the dome rises and the great shadow lies? The Cardinal's face has grown sharp and sunken in these hours; it is of a pallor like the ivory crucifix behind him. Round his lips lingers the unchanging inward smile of priesthood. His eyes beneath their drooping lids are intent—patient—menacing. His right hand is a little lifted with an unconscious movement of benediction: with such a gesture it is that the Pope—from above the portico of the Lateran—blesses the kneeling multitudes.

Max Beerbohm [1872–1956][41]

A Good Prince

I first saw him one morning of last summer, in the Green Park.

Though short, even insignificant, in stature and with an obvious tendency to be obese, he had that unruffled, Olympian air, which is so sure a sign of the Blood Royal. In a suit of white linen he looked serenely cool, despite the heat. Perhaps I should have thought him, had I not been versed in the *Almanach de Gotha,* a trifle older than he is. He did not raise his hat in answer to my salute, but smiled most graciously and made as though he would extend his hand to me, mistaking me, I doubt not, for one of his friends. A member of his suite, however, said something to him in an undertone, whereat he smiled again and took no further notice of me.

I do not wonder the people idolize him. His almost blameless life has been passed among them, nothing in it hidden from their knowledge. When they look upon his dear presentment in the photographer's window—the shrewd, kindly eyes under the high forehead, the sparse locks so carefully distributed—words of loyalty only and of admiration rise to their lips. For of all princes in modern days he seems to fulfill, most perfectly, the obligation of princely rank. Νήπιος* he might have been called in the heroic age, when princes were judged according to their mastery of the sword or of the bow, or have seemed, to those medieval eyes that loved to see a scholar's pate under the crown, an ignoramus. We are less exigent now. We do but ask of our princes that they should live among us, be often manifest to our eyes, set a perpetual example of a right life. We bid them be the ornaments of our State. Too often they do not attain to our ideal. They give, it may be, a half-hearted devotion to soldiering, or pursue pleasure merely—tales of their frivolity raising now and again the anger of a public swift to envy them their temptations. But against this admirable Prince no such charges can be made. Never (as yet, at least) has he cared to "play at soldiers." By no means has he shocked the Puritans. Though it is no secret that he prefers the society of ladies, not one breath of scandal has ever touched his name. Of how many English princes could this be said, in days when Figaro, quill in hand, inclines his ear to every key-hole?

Upon the one action that were well obliterated from his record I need not long insist. The wife of an aged ex-Premier came to have an audience and pay her respects. Hardly had she spoken, when His Royal Highness, in a fit of unreasoning displeasure, struck her a violent blow with his clenched fist. The incident is deplorable, but belongs, after all, to an earlier period of his life; and, were it not that no appreciation must rest upon the suppression of any scandal, I should not have referred to it. For the rest, I find no stain, soever faint, upon his life. The simplicity of his tastes is the more admirable for that he is known to care not at all for what may be reported in the newspapers. He has never touched a card, never entered a play-house. In no stud of racers has he indulged, preferring to the finest blood-horse ever bred a certain white and woolly lamb with a blue riband at its neck. This he is never tired of fondling. It is with him, like the roebuck of Henri Quatre, wherever he goes.

Suave and simple his life is! Narrow in range, it may be, but with every royal appurtenance of delight! Round the flower-garden at Sandringham runs an old wall of red brick, streaked with ivy and topped infrequently with balls of stone. By the iron gates, that open to a vista of flowers, stand two kind policemen, guarding the Prince's procedure along that bright vista. As his perambulator rolls out of the gate of St. James's Palace, he stretches out his tiny hands to the scarlet sentinels. An obsequious retinue follows him over the lawns of the White Lodge, cooing and laughing, blowing kisses and praising him. Yet his life has not been all happy. The afflictions that befall royal personages always touch very poignantly the heart of the people and it is not too much to say that all England watched by the cradle-side of Prince Edward in those hours of pain, when first the little battlements rose about the rose-red roof of his mouth. Irreiterate be the horror of that epoch!

As yet, when we know not even what his first words will be, it is too early to predict what verdict posterity will pass upon him. Already he has won the hearts of the people; but, in the years which, it is to be hoped, still await him, he may accomplish more. *Attendons!* He stands alone among European princes—but, as yet, only with the aid of a chair.

* Νήπιος [népios]: literally, an infant; an immature or simple-minded person.

Samuel P. Carrick, Jr. [1873–1930][42]

A Geological Parable

It was at the place afterwards called Solenhofen. The weather was miserable, as Jurassic weather usually was. The rain beat steadily down, and carbon dioxide was still upon the earth.

The Archaeopteryx was feeling pretty gloomy, for at that morning's meeting of the Amalgamated Association of Enaliosaurians he had been blackballed. He was looked down upon by the Pterodactyl and the Ichthyosaurus deigned not to notice him. Cast out by the Reptilia, and Aves not being thought of, he became a wanderer upon the face of the earth. "Alas!" sighed the poor Archaeopteryx, "this world is no place for me." And he laid him down and died; and became imbedded in the rock.

And ages afterward a featherless biped, called man, dug him up, and marveled at him, crying, "Lo, the original Avis and fountain-head of all our feathered flocks!" And they placed him with great reverence in a case, and his name became a by-word in the land. But the Archaeopteryx knew it not. And the descendant for whom be had suffered and died strutted proudly about the barn-yard, crowing lustily cock-a-doodle-do!

Yone Noguchi [1875–1947][43]

from The Summer Cloud: Prose Poems

I Hear the Wind Sighing

I hear the wind sighing underneath the Autumn grasses, I hear the wind sighing of the dying among the ebbing tide: underneath the Autumn grasses the dead spirit is resting, with the ebbing tide the tired fancies hurry away.

And also underneath the Autumn grasses, among the ebbing tide, alas, I see the shadow of my face—my own shadow sighing and sighing.

Here underneath the Shade of a Willow Tree

Here underneath the shade of a willow tree I sit. Isn't this willow tree a Bodhi tree under which solitary swing the Great Sage, Siddhartha, peacefully set his mind upon Truth and dream? Meditation! And Silence! The breeze passed by me in its graceful aerial gown. Isn't it the same breeze which passed through the Hindu forest some three thousand years ago? I said: "Oh, Spring solitude! Again I will lean upon this willow tree mine." Then the bell sounded from far-away. And again silence, and Silence,—the oldest and noblest language which unheard melody calms one's soul to dream.

My head bent down in prayer.

Something Must Happen

"Something must happen, 'tis high time," I said. All the voices gradually died into the fully-flowed bosom of the noonday. The sun is indolent; the earth is wrapped by the golden air: the butterflies flew away. The trees folded the shadows into their sleeves.

"Something must happen, 'tis high time," I said. The rivulet and the shadows of roses are still.

"Yes, something must happen, 'tis high time," I said.

An apple dropped suddenly to the ground.

Zitkála-Šá [Gertrude Simmons Bonnin, 1876–1938][44]

from Impressions of an Indian Childhood

My Mother

A wigwam of weather-stained canvas stood at the base of some irregularly ascending hills. A footpath wound its way gently down the sloping land till it reached the broad river bottom; creeping through the long swamp grasses that bent over it on either side, it came out on the edge of the Missouri.

Here, morning, noon, and evening, my mother came to draw water from the muddy stream for our household use. Always, when my mother started for the river, I stopped my play to run along with her. She was only of medium height. Often she was sad and silent, at which times her full arched lips were compressed into hard and bitter lines, and shadows fell under her black eyes. Then I clung to her hand and begged to know what made the tears fall.

"Hush; my little daughter must never talk about my tears"; and smiling through them, she patted my head and said, "Now let me see how fast you can run today." Whereupon I tore away at my highest possible speed, with my long black hair blowing in the breeze.

I was a wild little girl of seven. Loosely clad in a slip of brown buckskin, and light-footed with a pair of soft moccasins on my feet, I was as free as the wind that blew my hair, and no less spirited than a bounding deer. These were my mother's pride,—my wild freedom and overflowing spirits. She taught me no fear save that of intruding myself upon others.

Having gone many paces ahead I stopped, panting for breath, and laughing with glee as my mother watched my every movement. I was not wholly conscious of myself, but was more keenly alive to the fire within. It was as if I were the activity, and my hands and feet were only experiments for my spirit to work upon.

Returning from the river, I tugged beside my mother, with my hand upon the bucket I believed I was carrying. One time, on such a return, I remember a bit of conversation we had. My grown-up cousin, Warca-Ziwin (Sunflower), who was then seventeen, always went to the river alone for water for her mother. Their wigwam was not far from ours; and I saw her daily going to and from the river. I admired my cousin greatly. So I said: "Mother, when I am tall as my cousin Warca-Ziwin, you shall not have to come for water. I will do it for you."

With a strange tremor in her voice which I could not understand, she answered, "If the paleface does not take away from us the river we drink."

"Mother, who is this bad paleface?" I asked.

"My little daughter, he is a sham,—a sickly sham! The bronzed Dakota is the only real man."

I looked up into my mother's face while she spoke; and seeing her bite her lips, I knew she was unhappy. This aroused revenge in my small soul. Stamping my foot on the earth, I cried aloud, "I hate the paleface that makes my mother cry!"

Setting the pail of water on the ground, my mother stooped, and stretching her left hand out on the level with my eyes, she placed her other arm about me; she pointed to the hill where my uncle and my only sister lay buried.

"There is what the paleface has done! Since then your father too has been buried in a hill nearer the rising sun. We were once very happy. But the paleface has stolen our lands and driven us hither. Having defrauded us of our land, the paleface forced us away.

"Well, it happened on the day we moved camp that your sister and uncle were both very sick. Many others were ailing, but there seemed to be no help. We traveled many days and nights; not in the grand, happy way that we moved camp when I was a little girl, but we were driven, my child, driven like a herd of buffalo. With every step, your sister, who was not as large as you are now, shrieked with the painful jar until she was hoarse with crying. She grew more and more feverish. Her little hands and cheeks were burning hot. Her little lips were parched and dry, but she would not drink the water I gave her. Then I discovered that her throat was swollen and red. My poor child, how I cried with her because the Great Spirit had forgotten us!

"At last, when we reached this western country, on the first weary night your sister died. And soon your uncle died also, leaving a widow and an orphan daughter, your cousin Warca-Ziwin. Both your sister and uncle might have been happy with us today, had it not been for the heartless paleface."

My mother was silent the rest of the way to our wigwam. Though I saw no tears in her eyes, I knew that was because I was with her. She seldom wept before me.

The Dead Man's Plum Bush

One autumn afternoon many people came streaming toward the dwelling of our near neighbor. With painted faces, and wearing broad white bosoms of elk's teeth, they hurried down the narrow footpath to Haraka Wambdi's wigwam. Young mothers held their children by the hand, and half pulled them along in their haste. They overtook and passed by the bent old grandmothers who were trudging along with crooked canes toward the centre of excitement. Most of the young braves galloped hither on their ponies. Toothless warriors, like the old women, came more slowly, though mounted on lively ponies. They sat proudly erect on their horses. They wore their eagle plumes, and waved their various trophies of former wars.

In front of the wigwam a great fire was built, and several large black kettles of venison were suspended over it. The crowd were seated about it on the grass in a great circle. Behind them some of the braves stood leaning against the necks of their ponies, their tall figures draped in loose robes which were well drawn over their eyes.

Young girls, with their faces glowing like bright red autumn leaves, their glossy braids falling over each ear, sat coquettishly beside their chaperons. It was a custom for young Indian women to invite some older relative to escort them to the public feasts. Though it was not an iron law, it was generally observed.

Haraka Wambdi was a strong young brave, who had just returned from his first battle, a warrior. His near relatives, to celebrate his new rank, were spreading a feast to which the whole of the Indian village was invited.

Holding my pretty striped blanket in readiness to throw over my shoulders, I grew more and more restless as I watched the gay throng assembling. My mother was busily broiling a wild duck that my aunt had that morning brought over.

"Mother, mother, why do you stop to cook a small meal when we are invited to a feast?" I asked, with a snarl in my voice.

"My child, learn to wait. On our way to the celebration we are going to stop at Chanyu's wigwam. His aged mother-in-law is lying very ill, and I think she would like a taste of this small game."

Having once seen the suffering on the thin, pinched features of this dying woman, I felt a momentary shame that I had not remembered her before.

On our way I ran ahead of my mother and was reaching out my hand to pick some purple plums that grew on a small bush, when I was checked by a low "Sh!" from my mother.

"Why, mother, I want to taste the plums!" I exclaimed, as I dropped my hand to my side in disappointment.

"Never pluck a single plum from this bush, my child, for its roots are wrapped around an Indian's skeleton. A brave is buried here. While he lived he was so fond of playing the game of striped plum seeds that, at his death, his set of plum seeds were buried in his hands. From them sprang up this little bush."

Eyeing the forbidden fruit, I trod lightly on the sacred ground, and dared to speak only in whispers until we had gone many paces from it. After that time I halted in my ramblings whenever I came in sight of the plum bush. I grew sober with awe, and was alert to hear a long-drawn-out whistle rise from the roots of it. Though I had never heard with my own ears this strange whistle of departed spirits, yet I had listened so frequently to hear the old folks describe it that I knew I should recognize it at once.

The lasting impression of that day, as I recall it now, is what my mother told me about the dead man's plum bush.

The Ground Squirrel

In the busy autumn days my cousin Warca-Ziwin's mother came to our wigwam to help my mother preserve foods for our winter use. I was very fond of my aunt, because she was not so quiet as my mother. Though she was older, she was more jovial and less reserved. She was slender and remarkably erect. While my mother's hair was heavy and black, my aunt had unusually thin locks.

Ever since I knew her she wore a string of large blue beads around her neck,—beads that were precious because my uncle had given them to her when she was a younger woman. She had a peculiar swing in her gait, caused by a long stride rarely natural to so slight a figure. It was during my aunt's visit with us that my mother forgot her accustomed quietness, often laughing heartily at some of my aunt's witty remarks.

I loved my aunt threefold: for her hearty laughter, for the cheerfulness she caused my mother, and most of all for the times she dried my tears and held me in her lap, when my mother had reproved me.

Early in the cool mornings, just as the yellow rim of the sun rose above the hills, we were up and eating our breakfast. We awoke so early that we saw the sacred hour when a misty smoke hung over a pit surrounded by an impassable sinking mire. This strange smoke appeared every morning, both winter and summer; but most visibly in midwinter it rose immediately above the marshy spot. By the time the full face of the sun appeared above the eastern horizon, the smoke vanished. Even very old men, who had known this country the longest, said that the smoke from this pit had never failed a single day to rise heavenward.

As I frolicked about our dwelling I used to stop suddenly, and with a fearful awe watch the smoking of the unknown fires. While the vapor was visible I was afraid to go very far from our wigwam unless I went with my mother.

From a field in the fertile river bottom my mother and aunt gathered an abundant supply of corn. Near our tepee they spread a large canvas upon the grass, and dried their sweet corn in it. I was left to watch the corn, that nothing should disturb it. I played around it with dolls made of ears of corn. I braided their soft fine silk for hair, and gave them blankets as various as the scraps I found in my mother's workbag.

There was a little stranger with a black-and-yellow-striped coat that used to come to the drying corn. It was a little ground squirrel, who was so fearless of me that he came to one corner of the canvas and carried away as much of the sweet corn as he could hold. I wanted very much to catch him and rub his pretty fur back, but my mother said he would be so frightened if I caught him that he would bite my fingers. So I was as content as he to keep the corn between us. Every morning he came for more corn. Some evenings I have seen him creeping about our grounds; and when I gave a sudden whoop of recognition he ran quickly out of sight.

When mother had dried all the corn she wished, then she sliced great pumpkins into thin rings; and these she doubled and linked together into long chains. She hung them on a pole that stretched between two forked posts. The wind and sun soon thoroughly dried the chains of pumpkin. Then she packed them away in a case of thick and stiff buckskin.

In the sun and wind she also dried many wild fruits,—cherries, berries, and plums. But chiefest among my early recollections of autumn is that one of the corn drying and the ground squirrel.

I have few memories of winter days at this period of my life, though many of the summer. There is one only which I can recall.

Some missionaries gave me a little bag of marbles. They were all sizes and colors. Among them were some of colored glass. Walking with my mother to the river, on a late winter day, we found great chunks of ice piled all along the bank. The ice on the river was floating in huge pieces. As I stood beside one large block, I noticed for the first time the colors of the rainbow in the crystal ice. Immediately I thought of my glass marbles at home. With my bare fingers I tried to pick out some of the colors, for they seemed so near the surface. But my fingers began to sting with the intense cold, and I had to bite them hard to keep from crying.

From that day on, for many a moon, I believed that glass marbles had river ice inside of them.

Lord Dunsany [Edward Plunkett, 1878–1957][45]

from Time and the Gods

Usury

The men of Zonu hold that Yahn is God, who sits as a usurer behind a heap of little lustrous gems and ever clutches at them with both his arms. Scarce larger than a drop of water are the gleaming jewels that lie under the grasping talons of Yahn, and every jewel is a life. Men tell in Zonu that the earth was empty when Yahn devised his plan, and on it no life stirred. Then Yahn lured to him shadows whose home was beyond the Rim, who knew little of joys and nought of any sorrow, whose place was beyond the Rim before the birth of Time. These Yahn lured to him and showed them his heap of gems; and in the jewels there was light, and green fields glistened in them, and there were glimpses of blue sky and little streams, and very faintly little gardens showed that flowered in orchard lands. And some showed winds in the heaven, and some showed the arch of the sky with a waste plain drawn across it, with grasses bent in the wind and never aught but the plain. But the gems that changed the most had in their centre the ever changing sea. Then the shadows gazed into the Lives and saw the green fields and the sea and earth and the gardens of earth. And Yahn said: "I will loan you each a Life, and you may do your work with it upon the Scheme of Things and have each a shadow for his servant in green fields and in gardens, only for these things you shall polish these Lives with experience and cut their edges with your griefs, and in the end shall return them again to me."

And thereto the shadows consented, that they might have the gleaming Lives and have shadows for their servants, and this thing became the Law. But the shadows, each with his Life, departed and came to Zonu and to other lands, and there with experience they polished the Lives of Yahn, and cut them with human griefs until they gleamed anew. And ever they found new scenes to gleam within these Lives, and cities and sails and men shone in them where there had been before only green fields and sea, and ever Yahn the usurer cried out to remind them of their bargain. When men added to their Lives scenes that were pleasant to Yahn, then was Yahn silent, but when they added scenes that pleased not the eyes of Yahn, then did he take a toll of sorrow from them because it was the Law.

But men forgot the usurer, and there arose some claiming to be wise in the Law, who said that after their labor, which they wrought upon their Lives, was done, those Lives should be theirs to possess; so men took comfort from their toil and labour and the grinding and cutting of their griefs. But as their Lives began to shine with experience of many things, the thumb and forefinger of Yahn would suddenly close upon a Life, and the man became a shadow. But away beyond the Rim the shadows say:

"We have greatly laboured for Yahn, and have gathered griefs in the world, and caused his Lives to shine, and Yahn doeth nought for us. Far better had we stayed where no cares are, floating beyond the Rim."

And there the shadows fear lest ever again they be lured by specious promises to suffer usury at the hands of Yahn, who is overskilled in the Law. Only Yahn sits and smiles, watching his hoard increase in preciousness, and hath no pity for the poor shadows whom he hath lured from their quiet to toil in the form of men.

And ever Yahn lures more shadows and sends them to brighten his Lives, sending the old Lives out again to make them brighter still; and sometimes he gives to a shadow a Life that was once a king's and sendeth him with it down to the earth to play the part of a beggar, or sometimes he sendeth a beggar's Life to play the part of a king. What careth Yahn?

The men of Zonu have been promised by those that claim to be wise in the Law that their Lives which they have toiled at shall be theirs to possess forever, yet the men of Zonu fear that Yahn is greater and overskilled in the Law. Moreover it hath been said that Time will bring the hour when the wealth of Yahn shall be such as his dreams have lusted for. Then shall Yahn leave the earth at rest and trouble the shadows no more, but sit and gloat with his unseemly face over his hoard of Lives, for his soul is a usurer's soul. But others say, and they swear that this is true, that there are gods of Old, who be far greater than Yahn, who made the Law wherein Yahn is overskilled, and who will one day drive a bargain with him that shall be too hard for Yahn. Then Yahn shall wander away, a mean forgotten god, and perchance in some forsaken land shall haggle with the rain for a drop of water to drink, for his soul is a usurer's soul.

And the Lives—who knoweth the gods of Old or what Their will shall be?

Mlideen

Upon an evening of the forgotten years the gods were seated upon Mowrah Nawut above Mlideen holding the avalanche in leash.

All in the Middle City stood the Temples of the city's priests, and hither came all the people of Mlideen to bring them gifts, and there it was the wont of the City's priests to carve them gods for Mlideen. For in a room apart in the Temple of Eld in the midst of the temples that stood in the Middle City of Mlideen there lay a book called the Book of Beautiful Devices, writ in a language that no man may read and writ long ago, telling how a man may make for himself gods that shall neither rage nor seek revenge against a little people. And ever the priests came forth from reading in the Book of Beautiful Devices and ever they sought to make benignant gods, and all the gods that they made were different from each other, only their eyes turned all upon Mlideen.

But upon Mowrah Nawut for all of the forgotten years the gods had waited and forborne until the people of Mlideen should have carven one hundred gods. Never came lightnings from Mowrah Nawut crashing upon Mlideen, nor blight on harvests nor pestilence in the city, only upon Mowrah Nawut the gods sat and smiled. The people of Mlideen had said: "Yoma is god." And the gods sat and smiled. And after the forgetting of Yoma and the passing of years the people had said: "Zungari is god." And the gods sat and smiled.

Then on the altar of Zungari a priest had set a figure squat, carven in purple agate, saying "Yazun is god." Still the gods sat and smiled.

About the feet of Yonu, Bazun, Nidish and Sandrao had gone the worship of the people of Mlideen, and still the gods sat holding the avalanche in leash above the city.

There set a great calm towards sunset over the heights, and Mowrah Nawut stood up still with gleaming snow, and into the hot city cool breezes blew from his benignant slopes as Tarsi Zalo, high prophet of Mlideen, carved out of a great sapphire the city's hundredth god, and then upon Mowrah Nawut the gods turned away saying: "One hundred infamies have now been wrought." And they looked no longer upon Mlideen and held the avalanche no more in leash, and he leapt forward howling.

Over the Middle City of Mlideen now lies a mass of rocks, and on the rocks a new city is builded wherein people dwell who know not old Mlideen, and the gods are seated on Mowrah Nawut still. And in the new city men worship carven gods, and the number of the gods that they have carven is ninety and nine, and I, the prophet, have found a curious stone and go to carve it into the likeness of a god for all Mlideen to worship

Biographical Sketches
by Holly Iglesias

JOURDON ANDERSON, 1825–1907

When ex-slave Jourdon Anderson received a request from his old master, Colonel P.H. Anderson, to return to the plantation and help restore it from the ravages of the Civil War, he responded with a letter written in a satirical manner that some have found evocative of Mark Twain.

Anderson was born in Tennessee, where he worked on the Anderson property, married and had eleven children. In 1864, he was emancipated by the Union Army and eventually settled in Dayton, Ohio, where he worked as a coachman, servant, and church sexton. His "Letter from a Freedman to His Old Master" was dictated to his employer, who had it published in the *Cincinnati Commercial* in August, 1865, shortly after the end of the Civil War. The letter, reprinted in the *New York Daily Tribune* and *The Freedman's Book,* was read widely.

MAX BEERBOHM, 1872–1956

Essayist, satirist, and caricaturist Sir Henry Maximilian Beerbohm was born in London to a prosperous merchant family and educated at Oxford, where his scholarly performance was unremarkable. In his twenties, he became acquainted with Oscar Wilde and Aubrey Beardlsey and gained a reputation as a dandy and a humorist. Early essays—such as "A Defence of Cosmetics," an ironic defense of Decadence, and "The Incomparable Beauty of Modern Dress"—were published in London journals, and met with great enthusiasm for their highly mannered and amusing style. Wilde found his work "very precious and thought-out: quite delightfully wrong and fascinating."

Concluding a decade as art critic at the *Saturday Review,* Beerbohm moved with his wife, the American actress Florence Kahn, to Italy in 1910, where they lived for the remainder of their lives (except during the two world wars). His best known works include *Zuleika Dobson* (1911), his only novel; *A Christmas Garland* (1912), a collection of satires; *Seven Men* (1919), short stories; *And Even Now* (1920), essays; and *Mainly on the Air* (1946), a collection of his BBC broadcasts. He died in Rapallo, Italy and his ashes are interred at St. Paul's Cathedral in London.

WILLIAM BLAKE, 1757–1827

English poet, engraver, and painter, William Blake hardly needs introduction as an icon of early Romanticism. But he was also a harbinger of the modern, displaying in *The Marriage of Heaven and Hell* (1790) what the editor of this collection asserts is the "first use of the prose short in English as a self-conscious literary device."

A prophetic visionary, Blake revered the Bible but railed against the constraints of organized religion on the human imagination, which he considered the body of God. Sensitive to the pressures of a rapidly industrializing, often violent England, Blake envisioned cataclysmic changes while also yearning for spiritual union with the divine. Alexander Gilchrist, in his biography (1863), claimed that Blake wrote "for children and angels; himself 'a divine child,' whose playthings were sun, moon, and stars, the heavens and the earth."

Early poems were published in *Poetical Sketches* (1783), but after the death of his favorite brother, he practiced "illuminated writing," led by his brother's spirit, and published two collections of poems with engravings—*Songs of Innocence* (1789) and *Songs of Experience* (1794), with a title page announcing his intention to reveal "the two Contrary States of the Human Soul." *The Marriage of Heaven and Hell* also addresses the reconciliation of contrary states, reflecting Blake's response to the upheaval of his era.

GELETT BURGESS, 1866–1951

Illustrator, art critic, poet, and humorist, Gelett Burgess was born in Boston to a conservative New England family. After graduating from the Massachusetts Institute of Technology, he went to San Francisco where he taught topographical drawing at the University of California–Berkeley and immersed himself in the bohemian art scene. Eventually, he became important in the literary renaissance there in the 1890s, especially through the zany, eccentric little magazine, *The Lark*, which he published with William Doxey and Bruce Porter.

Burgess is remembered for introducing modern French art to America in his influential article "The Wild Men in Paris" (1910), published in *Architectural Record*. In addition to articles for popular magazines such as *The Smart Set*, *Collier's*, and *The Century*, he wrote nonsense verse such as "The Purple Cow" and the popular comic strip and book series, *Goops*, which taught children about manners: "The Goops they lick their fingers, / And the Goops they lick their knives; / They spill their broth on the tablecloth— / Oh, they lead disgusting lives!"

SAMUEL P. CARRICK, Jr., 1873–1930

Samuel Carrick was born in Nashville and moved with his family to Boston when he was a child. He was one of a handful of "baseball editors" (sports reporters) invited in 1912 to tour Fenway Park a few weeks before its official opening, and thus helped to introduce the new ballfield to the general public. At the time, Carrick wrote for the *Boston Journal,* but over a long career as a newspaperman, he worked for many papers and gained a reputation as one of the most well-informed baseball writers of his time. His obituary mentioned that he always worked at night, by choice, so that he would never miss a baseball game.

ROBERT W. CHAMBERS, 1865–1933

Robert Chambers was born in Brooklyn into a prominent family and was educated at the Brooklyn Polytechnic Institute, the Art Students' League, and in Paris for seven years at the École des Beaux-Arts and Académie Julian. Before he began to write fiction, he published illustrations in national magazines. His first novel, *In the Quarter* (1887), was followed by his most notable work, *The King in Yellow* (1895), a collection of short stories based on the supernatural.

While he continued to publish in this genre, he also turned to writing historical romances, adventure and war stories, and children's books. Though more a popularizer who mirrored society's tastes than a master stylist or innovator, Chambers was one of the most prolific and successful writers of his day. Much of his work was serialized in magazines such as *McCall's, The Woman's Home Companion,* and *Cosmopolitan,* thus reaching a broad audience. His novel, *The Tracer of Lost Persons* (1906), was adapted for radio, a crime drama that ran from 1937 to 1954.

KATE CHOPIN, 1850–1904

Kate O'Flaherty Chopin was born in St. Louis to a successful Irish immigrant father and a mother from a prominent family. While her early literary reputation was based on local-color writing, it later became apparent that she was a major Southern feminist writer, tackling taboo subjects and challenging standard notions of female sexuality.

She excelled as a student, reading classic and contemporary European writers in French and German, and graduated from the Academy of the Sacred Heart. In 1870, she married Oscar Chopin, settling first in New Orleans, then in rural Cloutierville, Louisiana. By 1879, the year in which her husband's cotton brokerage failed, she had born six children. Following his death, depressed and burdened with considerable debt, she returned to St. Louis in 1884. A family doctor suggested she write, not just for its therapeutic effects, but also as a source of income and a way to channel her considerable intellectual energy.

By the 1890s, Chopin's short stories began to appear in national magazines and were followed by the publication of *Bayou Folk* (1894), *A Night in Acadie* (1897), and *The Awakening* (1899), her most enduring work—although considered "unseemly" at the time. She became a significant figure in the cultural life of St. Louis, where she died in 1904, having suffered a cerebral hemorrhage at the Louisiana Purchase Exposition. She was largely forgotten until a revival of interest in her work was sparked by second-wave feminism in the 1970s.

ADA CLARE [JANE MCELHENNEY], 1834–1874

American writer and actress Ada Agnes Jane McElhenney was born in Charleston to an aristocratic Southern family. Around age eighteen, she began her writing career, first under the name Ada, and then Ada Clare and Alastor. In 1854 she moved to New York to work as an actress and became known as the Queen of Bohemia, frequenting Pfaff's Cellar, a rathskeller that was a hub of revolutionary arts culture. She was involved in a widely publicized affair with popular pianist and composer Louis Moreau Gottschalk, and bore him a son.

Walt Whitman considered Clare "the ideal of the modern woman: talented, intelligent, and emancipated." She wrote a regular column, "Thoughts and Things," for the arts weekly, the *Saturday Press*, and published one novel, *Only a Woman's Heart*, which was not well received. Crushed by the novel's failure, she returned to acting in a touring stock company. In 1868 she married actor Frank Noyes. She died of rabies several years later after suffering a dog bite in her theatrical agent's office. Poet Charles Stoddard eulogized her: "The queen is dead; but who shall cry 'Long live the Queen!' in her stead? Are there no more queens of Bohemia, I wonder, and is the Bohemia of that day a thing of the past, dead and gone forever?"

STEPHEN CRANE, 1871–1900

Poet, short story writer, journalist, and novelist, Stephen Crane was one of the great literary innovators of his generation, and his work had a strong influence on the Modernist experiments of the early twentieth century. Crane's approach put more emphasis on the drama of characters' inner lives than on plot and exposition, substituting imagistic and metaphorical representation for traditional description.

The fourteenth child born to Mary Helen and Jonathan Crane, a Methodist minister, Crane was educated at a seminary and a military school, as well as Syracuse University, where he was an erratic student but an ardent writer of short stories and sketches. By 1891, he had left college to be a full-time writer and reporter, a life full of adventure and excitement, and ultimately of danger and illness as well. He reported for newspapers and magazines on a wide variety of subjects, such as poverty in New York tenements, the Spanish American and Greco-Turkish wars, African exploration, coal mining, and Civil War battlefields.

Exceptionally precocious, he produced many enduring works in his twenties—his first novel, *Maggie: A Girl of the Streets* (1893), published under the pseudonym Johnston Smith; his first book of poems, *The Black Riders* (1895); the still popular masterpiece, *The Red Badge of Courage* (1895); *George's Mother* (1896); and *The Open Boat and Other Tales of Adventure* (1898). Months shy of his twenty-ninth birthday, he died of acute tuberculosis at a sanitarium in Germany and is buried in Hillside, New Jersey.

MARY MAPES DODGE, 1831–1905

Born into a prominent New York family, Mary Mapes Dodge rose to prominence as a bestselling author and editor of newspapers and periodicals. She grew up in a happy home, well educated and exposed to literary luminaries of the day. After she married and had two children, the new family moved into her husband's multi-generational home in New York City. Though living in comfort as an urban, middle-class wife, tragedy struck when her husband drowned in 1858. She returned to Waverly, New Jersey, to live with her parents and sisters on an old farmstead. There she educated her sons and pursued her many interests—skating, music, swimming, printing, collecting natural specimens.

Always close to her father, she assisted him with the publication of the *Working Farmer* and the *United States Journal*, writing many of the articles and using a variety of names and initials to give the impression of several authors. Encouraged by the response to her writing, she began to contribute stories to *Harper's New Monthly Magazine.* At her father's behest, she wrote a popular collection, *The Irvington Stories* (1864), followed by her most famous work, the novel, *Hans Brinker; or, The Silver Skates* (1865). She began a formidable editing career in 1866 as the associate editor of the weekly *Hearth and Home,* and subsequently as an editor in her own right of *St. Nicholas Magazine,* considered to be the most influential children's publication of the late nineteenth century.

ERNEST DOWSON, 1867–1900

Poet, short story writer, playwright, critic, translator, and novelist, Ernest Dowson was born in London to a cultured merchant family and was educated at home, abroad, and finally at Oxford. He worked at his father's dry-docking business but his primary occupations as a young adult were writing and a bawdy social life. To many, he represents the archetypal Decadent artist, known as much for his lifestyle as for his creations, a self-destructive, tortured individual pursuing an impossible ideal.

He preferred writing prose, keenly aware of its poetic possibilities, and wrote in a lyrical, emotionally-laden mode. He collaborated on two novels with Arthur Moore—*A Comedy of Masks* (1893) and *Adrian Rome* (1899)—published several collections of poems and short stories, as well as the one-act play, *The Pierrot of the Minute* (1897), and worked on a novel that was never finished, *Madame de Viole*. In addition, Dowson was a prolific translator of French fiction, including work by Zola and Balzac.

After the death of his parents, his life began to deteriorate, physically and financially, despite his growing literary reputation. He died of advanced tuberculosis, nearly penniless, in the home of a friend. Upon his death, Oscar Wilde wrote, "Poor wounded wonderful fellow . . . a tragic reproduction of all tragic poetry, like a symbol, or a scene."

LORD DUNSANY [EDWARD PLUNKETT], 1878–1957

Born in London to a wealthy and fabled Anglo-Irish family, fiction writer, essayist, poet, and dramatist, Edward Plunkett was educated at Cheam School, Eton College, and the Royal Military Academy at Sandhurst. He served in the Boer War and World War I, after which he pursued a literary career in the British tradition of the "gentleman amateur." The title of 18th Baron of Dunsany passed to him upon the death of his father in 1899, and he published under the name Lord Dunsany.

A prolific writer, he published novels, autobiographies, plays, translations, and hundreds of short stories. Two novels, *The Chronicles of Rodrigo* (1922) and *The King of Elfland's Daughter* (1924), are acclaimed as classics of fantasy literature. Although he began his literary career with short stories, his first notoriety came through his association with the Abbey Theatre in Dublin, where his early play, *The Glittering Gate* (1909), was produced. Throughout his life, he continued to produce work in all genres and was praised for his sonorous, evocative language and his highly crafted style.

RALPH WALDO EMERSON, 1803–1882

For influence in shaping a distinctly American philosophy, Ralph Waldo Emerson has no peer, forever linked to concepts such as individualism, egalitarianism, self-reliance, and the glorification of nature. After graduation from Harvard Divinity School, he married and assumed a pastorship, though plagued by doubts regarding Christian doctrine. The death of his young wife in 1831 led to a period of grief and withdrawal, followed by travel to Europe where he met Carlyle and Wordsworth.

Returning to Concord, he married again and began a lifelong career as a public lecturer. Traditional Protestantism behind him, he underwent an intense spiritual awakening enriched by immersion in Eastern cultural texts, becoming convinced that the individual soul was identical with the divine.

His groundbreaking treatise, *Nature* (1836), sparked the New England Transcendentalist movement, much of its philosophy disseminated in the pages of the influential magazine *The Dial* (1840–1844). Serving a stint as editor, Emerson was instrumental in introducing American audiences to the literature, philosophy and religion of the East.

He continued to lecture, edit anthologies, and publish essays and poems throughout his long and distinguished life. His most influential essays continue to be anthologized, including "Self-Reliance," "Compensation," "The Over-Soul," "Circles," "The Poet," "Experience," "Politics," "New England Reformers," and "The American Scholar."

ALCÉE FORTIER, 1856–1914

Author, educator, and translator, Alcée Fortier was born in Louisiana to a distinguished French Creole family whose sugar-plantation fortune was significantly diminished by the outcome of the Civil War. He obtained a classical education at the school of A. V. Romain in New Orleans and attended the University of Virginia until he became too ill to continue. Returning to New Orleans, he read law and clerked for several years before teaching French in the city high school.

His true calling, however, began with his appointment as Professor of Romance Languages at Tulane University, where he spent his entire career, expanding his area of expertise from European languages to Acadian French, Louisiana Creole, and folklore of Acadians and freedmen. In addition, he served as president of the Modern Language Association and the Louisiana Historical Society.

Fortier's output was prodigious, even as he continued his teaching and public service work. Among his important works are *Sept Grand Auteurs du Dix-neuvième Siècle* (1889), *Histoire de la Littérature Française* (1893), *Louisiana Folk Tales: In French Dialect and English Translation* (1895), *A History of Louisiana* (1903), and the novella, *Gabriel d'Ennerich, Histoire d'un Cadet de Famille au XVIIIe Siècle* (1886).

CHARLOTTE PERKINS GILMAN, 1860–1935

Feminist writer, editor, and lecturer, Charlotte Perkins Gilman was born in Hartford to a prominent family of intellectuals and social activists. Although her father abandoned the family soon after her birth and provided only meager financial support, Perkins inherited some property in 1874, allowing her to attend private school and then the Rhode Island School of Design. She married artist Walter Stetson in 1884 and had a daughter, the birth causing severe postpartum depression, which was treated with the "rest cure"—total withdrawal from social, physical and intellectual activity—the experience described in excruciating detail in "The Yellow Wallpaper" (1892). She and Stetson separated in 1888, at which time she moved with her daughter to California, where she became active in reformist groups.

1898 saw the publication of the acclaimed *Women and Economics,* which was expanded upon in *The Home: Its Work and Influence* (1903), calling for a change in women's status as dependents who pay off their economic debts through sex and maternal nurturing. In 1900, she married Houghton Gilman, an attorney who was her first cousin, and they lived in New York City. In addition to poetry, short stories, journalism, and sociology, she wrote several utopian novels, including *Moving the Mountain* (1911) and *Herland* (serialized in 1915, published in book form in 1979).

A proponent of euthanasia, Gilman committed suicide 1935 after several years of battling cancer.

NATHANIEL HAWTHORNE, 1803–1864

Romantic short-story writer and novelist, Nathaniel Hawthorne was deeply rooted in New England, having one ancestor who was a member of the Massachusetts Bay Colony, another a judge at the Salem witch trials. His writing explores Puritanism and the dark themes of ancestral guilt, vengeance, and sin. Master of a simple and direct style, Hawthorne nonetheless larded his tales and sketches with symbology.

In 1836, he served a brief stint as editor of the *American Magazine of Useful and Entertaining Knowledge,* followed the next year by publication of *Twice-Told Tales.* He was appointed to a position at the Boston custom house, but it allowed no time for writing, causing him to resign after two years and move to Brook Farm, the utopian communal experiment.

Hawthorne married in 1842 and moved into the Old Manse in Concord. During this time he published short stories such as "The Birthmark" and "Rappaccini's Daughter," demonstrating his keen ability to delineate human character. With notable Transcendentalists as neighbors, he was in fine intellectual company, although his affinity was primarily with Thoreau, with whom he frequently took long walks.

For years, the family's fortune vacillated, Hawthorne's jobs vulnerable to the spoils system, taking them from place to place. A prolonged retreat in the Berkshires, however, proved productive and lucrative, seeing the publication of *The Scarlet Letter* (1850), *The House of the Seven Gables* (1851) and *The Blithedale Romance* (1852). Hawthorne died in 1864 while touring the White Mountains.

LAFCADIO HEARN, 1850–1904

Lafcadio Hearn—restless flâneur, connoisseur of the exotic, journalist, critic, translator of Anatole France and Guy de Maupassant—was born in Greece to an Irish father and a Greek mother during the British occupation. He endured an insecure childhood, abandoned at an early age by both parents and left in the care of an aunt in Ireland. At nineteen, he was given a one-way ticket to New York—"dropped moneyless on the pavement of an American city to begin life"—and found his way to Cincinnati.

Hearn performed menial jobs, spent many hours in the public library and eventually found work as a reporter, gaining a reputation for sensationalistic crime stories as well as sensitive coverage of the poor. In 1877, he moved to New Orleans, where he lived for nearly a decade, writing for national magazines the characteristic sketches of Creole life for which he is renowned, miniatures of sight and scent, sound and mood .

In 1890, he went to Japan, where at long last he found a home. He married Koizumi Setsu, accepted a teaching position in Tokyo, became a Japanese citizen (under the name Koizumi Yakumo), and had four children. As he had with New Orleans, Hearn introduced the culture of Japan to a wider audience. His books include: *Gleanings in Buddha-Fields* (1897), *Japanese Fairy Tales* (1898), *Kwaidan: Stories and Studies of Strange Things* (1903), *Gombo Zhèbes: A Little Dictionary of Creole Proverbs* (1885), and *Creole Sketches* (1924).

RICHARD H. HORNE, 1802–1884

After Romanticism's first bloom, Richard Horne sought a new aesthetic approach, experimenting with genre, subject, and technique. Though not a lasting figure among British poets, he is distinguished by his copious work as a journalist, playwright, novelist, critic, and editor. He attended the Royal Military Academy but received no commission, eventually accepting a post in the Mexican navy, fighting for independence against Spain. In 1827 he returned to London, traveling first throughout Canada and the United States.

Back in England, he turned to literature as a profession, writing several plays, editing the *Monthly Repository* and *Dickens's Household Words,* and serving on the commission on child labor. A widely-read epic poem, *Orion,* was published in 1843 as well as a volume of critical essays, *A New Spirit of the Age.*

In 1852, Horne emigrated to Australia where he worked in many fields—the gold trade, labor arbitration, land speculation, and a vineyard that still exists as the Tahbilk Winery. These experiences were described in *Australian Facts and Prospects,* published in 1859. The following year he returned to London. Of his many books, the one that drew the most public interest was the collection of Elizabeth Barrett Browning's extensive correspondence with him.

JAMES G. HUNEKER, 1857–1921

Born in Philadelphia to a middle-class family that loved music, art, and theater, James Huneker received seven years of private-school education at the Broad Street Academy, where he excelled in French and literature. Instead of following his father's wish that he become a lawyer, or his mother's that he become a priest, he studied piano, eventually teaching it and writing music journalism.

Huneker moved to New York in 1886 and began a fifteen-year run at the *Musical Courier,* writing a column of critiques, stories, news, and anecdotes as "Raconteur." From 1889 until his death, he served as a contributor for nearly a dozen newspapers and magazines, becoming one of the most versatile and esteemed critics, covering art, literature, drama, and music with insight and verve. He introduced the reading public to such budding greats as Debussy, Ibsen, Strindberg, Matisse, Joyce, Shaw, and Cézanne.

The well-received book, *Iconoclasts: a Book of Dramatists* (1905), confirmed Huneker's reputation as a literary and drama critic and remained a bestseller for many years. Other important works, of criticism and memoir, include *Egoists: A Book of Supermen* (1909), *The Pathos of Distance: A Book of a Thousand and One Moments* (1913), *Ivory Apes and Peacocks* (1915), *Unicorns* (1917), and *Steeplejack* (1920).

LEIGH HUNT, 1784–1859

While not considered one of the greats of British Romantic poetry, Leigh Hunt was a central figure of that movement and produced many poems in a variety of forms, as well as translations of Italian, French, Greek, and Roman poets. Today he is primarily remembered for his long poem, *The Story of Rimini* (1816), written while serving a prison term for slandering the Prince Regent. Nonetheless, his influence as an essayist, editor, and critic were considerable during his time.

Hunt is credited with introducing the public to major literary lights of the nineteenth century—Tennyson, Shelley, Browning—and offering encouragement to the likes of Lamb, Dickens, and Hazlitt. In his day, he was a noted journalist and influential editor of newspapers, such as the *Examiner,* and numerous arts journals. He also wrote a novel and several plays, two of which were produced.

His marriage was not a happy one, with many children and never enough money. One son felt that his mother's sister Elizabeth was better suited to his father, being quite bright and literary and probably in love with him. Hunt is buried in London, his wife on one side and her sister on the other.

HARRIET JACOBS, 1813–1897

Author and abolitionist reformer, Harriet Jacobs escaped from slavery, capturing the experience of bondage and flight in the personal narrative, *Incidents in the Life of a Slave Girl.* The book, published under the name Linda Brent, shed light on the dilemma of female slaves who suffered from sexual predation and the inability to protect their children. Conflicted about revealing the sexual aspect of her story, she believed it worth telling: "If it could help save another from my fate, it would be selfish and unchristian in me to keep it back."

In 1835, Jacobs fled her master's home, and hid for seven years in her grandmother's attic. In 1842 she escaped to the North, working as a nursemaid and in the abolitionist movement, first in Philadelphia, then in Rochester, New York. Her first published work was a letter, signed "Fugitive," to the *New York Tribune* (1853), contesting former First Lady Julia Tyler's defense of slavery.

While she continued writing letters to newspapers, she also began work on *Incidents in the Life of a Slave Girl,* which was first published in 1861, reaching a large, primarily white, Christian, female audience. During the Civil War and Reconstruction, Jacobs raised funds to feed, clothe and shelter refugee slaves and poor free blacks, organizing communities around the South to build hospitals, schools, churches and homes. She died in 1897 and was buried in bucolic Mount Auburn Cemetery in Cambridge, Massachusetts, where her headstone reads: "Patient in tribulation, fervent in spirit serving the Lord."

GRACE KING, 1852–1932

Daughter of a prosperous lawyer, Grace King grew up in a genteel home and was educated in convent schools in New Orleans. The family, however, fled the city to their plantation to wait out the Civil War, returning to New Orleans at its conclusion only to live in relative poverty. She was determined to rise above these reduced circumstances through travel and writing, visiting New England, England, and France, and making the acquaintance of such greats as Mark Twain, who became a close friend, and William Dean Howells.

Her first publication, the short story, "Monsieur Motte" (1886), set some of the themes and characters that recur throughout her work—feminine solidarity in the face of adversity, loyal black servants, and lost fathers and husbands. *Tales of Time and Place* (1892), a collection of five stories, was followed by the critically acclaimed *Balcony Stories* (1893; republished in 1914 and 1925), a local-color model of a lyrically reconstructed past. In addition to fiction, King wrote several histories, including *New Orleans: The Place and the People* (1895) and *DeSoto and His Men in the Land of Florida* (1898), and a memoir, *Memories of a Southern Woman of Letters* (1932).

EMMA LAZARUS, 1849–1887

Emma Lazarus, one of the first successful and highly visible Jewish writers in America, was the author of "The New Colossus" (1883), a sonnet that became iconic when lines from it were inscribed on the base of the Statue of Liberty. The poem inspired many, including Rose Hawthorne Lathrop, daughter of Nathaniel Hawthorne, who established an order of nuns to care for people without financial resources suffering from terminal cancer.

Lazarus was born into a large Sephardic-Ashkenazi family in New York, and showed an interest in literature and languages at an early age; her first collection, *Poems and Translations* (1867), was published in her teens. In addition to poetry, she wrote essays, fiction, and plays. Reading George Eliot's *Daniel Deronda* sparked Lazarus' interest in her own heritage, taking up the cause against persecution of the Jews in Russia in the pamphlet, *The Century* (1882), and exploring issues of Jewish-American identity in *Songs of a Semite: The Dance to Death and Other Poems* (1882).

An early Zionist, Lazarus was also a proponent of the political economics of Henry George, writing a poem that took its title from his popular work, *Progress and Poverty.* She participated in the establishment of the Hebrew Technical Institute in New York City, which provided vocational training to Jewish immigrants. Her home is included on the map of Women's Rights Historic Sites and she is buried in Beth-Olam Cemetery in Brooklyn.

FIONA MACLEOD [WILLIAM SHARP], 1855–1905

Scotsman William Sharp, described by his wife as "a Viking in build, a Scandinavian in cast of mind, a Celt in heart and spirit," was a prolific poet, critic, editor, novelist, playwright, and biographer. But it is the work penned after 1894 under the name Fiona Macleod that earned him an enduring reputation as the chief architect of a Celtic Twilight literature in Scotland.

The son of a prosperous mercantile family, he attended Glasgow University and later began contributing poems and articles to various newspapers, building a reputation that admitted him to literary circles which included such luminaries as Rossetti, Pater, Stevenson, Wilde, and Yeats. In the 1880s, he published his first poetry volume, *The Human Inheritance, The New Hope, Motherhood* (1882), followed by a series of biographies—of Rossetti, Heine, Shelley, Keats, and Browning—and two novels, *The Sport of Chance* (1888) and *Children of Tomorrow: A Romance* (1889).

The novel, *Pharais: A Romance of the Isles* (1894), introduced Sharp's alter ego, Fiona Macleod, and was followed by more than a dozen Fiona novels and short-story collections, each a mix of fantasy and naturalism, with a heroine who, like the writer's feminist persona, is an idealized earth mother.

Even as he turned out fiction, Sharp produced nonfiction such as *Progress of Art in the Century* (1902) and *Literary Geography* (1904). Overworked and in poor health, Sharp and his wife spent time in Sicily, where he died and is buried, his words marking the grave: "Farewell to the known and exhausted, / Welcome the unknown and illimitable."

DORA GREENWELL McCHESNEY, 1871–1912

Dora Greenwell McChesney was born in Illinois but traveled as a child throughout Europe with her mother, who educated her through broad reading and study of Italian art and Roman antiquities. Eventually she settled in England in a cottage on the Essex coast where she wrote historical fiction, favoring heroes defending lost causes. Among her books are *Kathleen Clare, Her Book, 1637–1641* (1895), *Miriam Cromwell, Royalist* (1897), *Beatrix Infelix: A Summer Tragedy in Rome* (1898), *Rupert, by the Grace of God: The Story of an Unrecorded Plot* (1899), *London Roses* (poems, 1903), *Cornet Strong of Ireton's Horse* (1913), and *The Confession of Richard Plantagenet* (1913).

FLORENCE A. MERRIAM [BAILEY], 1863–1948

One of the most literary ornithologists (whose words were "as sprightly and graceful as the birds themselves"), Florence Merriam Bailey introduced the modern tradition of field guides that draw on experience of living birds in the field rather than on examination of specimens in collections. Her *Birds Through an Opera-Glass* (1890), aimed at young people and women, was the first example of such a book, utilizing field notes first published in *Audubon Magazine.* Other work using this new approach include the books *Birds of Village and Field* (1898) and *Handbook of Birds of the Western United States* (1902), and articles in *Auk, Bird-Lore,* and *Condor.*

Bailey was born in upstate New York and was encouraged by her parents to study natural history. After attending Smith College, she established several chapters of the nascent National Audubon Society, and became active in the movement to prevent the slaughter of birds hunted for their decorative feathers, which contributed to the passage of a wildlife protection act in 1900. She married Vernon Bailey, chief naturalist for the U.S. Biological Survey, and traveled extensively with him, resulting in many collaborative projects, including *Wild Animals of Glacier National Park* (1918). For *Birds of New Mexico* (1928), she became the first woman to be awarded the Brewster Medal, the American Ornithologists' Union's highest honor.

YONE NOGUCHI, 1875–1947

Essayist, novelist, and poet, Yone Noguchi was the first Japanese-born writer to publish poetry in English and was a precursor of the Imagists. He left Japan in 1893 and worked as a journalist in San Francisco for several years. Eventually he discovered his true vocation under the encouragement of poet Joaquin Miller, who introduced him to the bohemian life of the Bay area. His first poems were published in 1896 in *The Lark*, the little magazine out of San Francisco edited by Gelett Burgess, and his first collection, *Seen and Unseen, or the Monologues of a Homeless Snail*, was released the following year.

Noguchi moved to New York in 1900 and began work on a novel with the help of an editor, Léonie Gilmour, who became his lover and the mother of his son, the sculptor Isamu Noguchi, though the relationship did not endure. The novel, *The American Diary of a Japanese Girl*, was published in 1904, the year he returned to Japan and became an important interpreter of Japanese culture to Westerners (and vice versa) as an international lecturer. *The Pilgrimage* (1909), a poetry collection, and *Through the Torii* (1913), a collection of essays, were well received, but by the 1920s his work had fallen out of favor and his politics grew increasingly anti-Western. His home was destroyed in 1945 by the American bombing of Tokyo, and he died of cancer in 1947.

MARY ALICIA OWEN, 1858–1935

Folklorist Mary Alicia Owen was born into a slave-owning family in St. Joseph, Missouri, when it was still a small, frontier town. While she listened intently to stories and conversations among slaves and Native Americans, her inspiration to record the disappearing tales was *Algonquin Legends* (1884), by Charles Godfrey Leland, with whom she began a long-term correspondence. He wrote the introduction to her first book, *Old Rabbit the Voodoo, and Other Sorcerers* (1893). The work for which she is best known is *Voodoo Tales as Told Among the Negroes of the Southwest* (1893). In addition to her research, she published (as Julia Scott) articles in *Overland Monthly* and *Century Magazine*, and served for many years as president of the Missouri Folklore Society.

ELIZABETH STUART PHELPS, 1844–1911

Daughter of a Congregationalist minister and a children's author, early American feminist Elizabeth Stuart Phelps grew up in an intellectual, religious household. Though baptized as Mary Grey Phelps, she wrote under the pseudonym of her mother's name, who died when she was eight. Over the course of her career, she published fifty-seven volumes of poetry, fiction, and essays that challenged gender roles and Christian notions of the afterlife.

A formally educated, precocious child, she had a story published in *Youth's Companion* at thirteen, another in *Harper's Magazine* at nineteen, and was acknowledged as a great talent early on by literary greats such as Thomas Wentworth Higginson and John Greenleaf Whittier. In adult life, she published children's books as well as adult fiction and essays, including the Gypsy Breynton series (1866–67), wildly popular spiritualist novels such as *The Gates Ajar* (1868), the feminist novel, *The Story of Avis* (1877), the antivivisection novel, *Trixy* (1904), and an autobiography, *A Singular Life* (1895).

She was also a popular lecturer, advocating social reform, temperance and women's emancipation, examining the power dynamics of patriarchal culture and delivering a powerful critique of the effects of marriage on women's creativity and their ability to live fulfilling lives. Expressing her ethics and aesthetics, she wrote that "the province of the artist is to portray life as it is; and life is moral responsibility."

EDGAR ALLAN POE, 1809–1849

A crucial figure in American Romanticism, Poe is unusual among writers of his era for having been able to support himself primarily through writing. He is best known for his poetry and short stories, especially those shrouded in the mysterious and the morbid, and was also an influential literary critic and journalist. Stories such as "The Tell-Tale Heart," "The Pit and the Pendulum," and "The Masque of the Red Death," and poems like "The Raven," "Annabel Lee," and "Lenore," continue to be anthologized and to haunt contemporary readers.

Orphaned at two, Poe was taken from Boston to Richmond to be raised by John and Frances Allan, with whom he lived into young adulthood. He briefly served in the U.S. Army, during which time his first book, *Tamerlane and Other Poems* (1827), was published under the byline, "A Bostonian." After military service, he began his career as a writer in earnest, editing and publishing in various magazines and newspapers. In 1836 he married his thirteen-year-old cousin, Virginia Clemm, followed by the publication of *The Narrative of Arthur Gordon Pym of Nantucket*, his only novel, and *Tales of the Grotesque and Arabesque.*

In the early 1840s, his wife became an invalid and Poe began to drink more heavily. His poem, "The Raven" (1845), was immediately popular and made

Poe a household name—despite the fact that he received only nine dollars for it. He followed this with an analysis of the poem's creation, "The Philosophy of Composition." In 1847 his wife died of consumption—after which he became more and more unstable, and died in 1849 under mysterious circumstances.

BRUCE PORTER, 1865–1953

Bruce Porter was a man of many talents—painter, sculptor, muralist, art critic, poet, stained-glass designer, landscape designer. He was raised in the East Bay area of San Francisco, where his father edited a local newspaper. He was educated there, as well as in Paris, London, and Venice. Porter wrote art criticism for newspapers and from 1895 to 1897 published the literary magazine, *The Lark,* with Gelett Burgess and William Doxey. He was a contributor to *Arts in California* (1916), a compilation of works on display at the Panama-Pacific International Exposition, including his tonalist painting, *Presidio Cliffs.* In 1917, he married Margaret James, daughter of Harvard philosopher and psychologist William James. His many stained glass windows, monuments, and gardens, including those at the renowned Filoli estate, can be seen throughout California.

HARRISON G. RHODES, 1871–1929

Born in Cleveland, Ohio, Harrison Garfield Rhodes was educated in public schools and at Western Reserve University and Harvard. He published many books, including *The Lady and the Ladder* (1905), *The Flight to Eden* (1907), *The Adventures of Charles Edward* (1908), *In Vacation America* (1915), *American Towns and People* (1920), and *High Life and Other Stories* (1920). In addition, he was the assistant editor of the magazine, *The Chap-Book,* one of the first and best-known "little magazines" in America.

DANTE GABRIEL ROSSETTI, 1828–1882

Poet, painter, translator, and illustrator, Dante Gabriel Rossetti was born in London into a highly cultured Italian expatriate family. He began translating Dante and medieval German poetry while attending Cary's Academy of Art in preparation for the Royal Academy. In 1848 he formed the Pre-Raphaelite Brotherhood with six other painters also interested in poetry, taking to task the stale conventions of the art academy, proposing instead a return to the vibrancy of painting in the Quattrocento.

Rossetti was greatly affected by the mid-century Anglo-Catholic revival, evidenced in religious or noble subjects that carry a message of moral reform, such as the painting, *The Girlhood of Mary Virgin,* and the allegorical prose tale, *Hand and Soul* (both from 1849). In 1862, the loss of a child and subsequent suicide of his young wife, Eleanor Siddal, pushed Rossetti into depression despite his growing popularity. By the end of the 1860s he was deeply involved in a complex relationship with Jane Burden Morris, the wife of William Morris, with whom Rossetti had founded a design firm. His portraits of her are considered to be among his most notable achievements, and his time involved with her yielded a formidable poetic output—seventeen "House of Life" sonnets, other ekphrastic sonnets, and the erotic "Troy Town" and "Eden Bower" in 1869 alone.

1881 saw the sale of *Dante's Dream,* one of his largest paintings, and the publication of the well received *Poems and Ballads and Sonnets.* The following year, he suffered a rapid decline in health, dying of blood poisoning on April 9.

HENRY R. SCHOOLCRAFT, 1793–1864
JANE JOHNSTON SCHOOLCRAFT, 1800–1842

Henry Schoolcraft was a geologist, ethnologist, geographer, Indian agent, and territorial legislator famed for his expedition to the source of the Mississippi River and his six-volume study of Native Americans, commissioned by Congress in 1850 and celebrated for its extensively researched scholarship.

He worked closely with his wife Jane Johnston, daughter of an Ojibwa mother and Scots-Irish father, whom he met while working as an Indian agent in Michigan. Her knowledge of the native language and legends, as well as the prominence of her cultured, wealthy family, opened many doors for him. Longfellow found source material for his long poem, "The Song of Hiawatha," in their translated stories.

Jane Schoolcraft's literary talent as a poet and storyteller was considerable, though her work circulated through only one magazine, *The Literary Voyager or Muzzeniegun.* Intended for the local residents of Sault Ste. Marie, the magazine was also distributed in Detroit and New York City, containing articles on Ojibwe traditions and customs and biographies of contemporary Native Americans. She died before her husband, after which he married Mary Howard, from a South Carolina slaveholding family.

After Henry died, his second wife gave more than two hundred of his books, published in thirty-five different Native American languages, to the Boston Athenaeum. His papers are archived at the Library of Congress. Jane Johnston Schoolcraft's work has recently been collected in *The Sound the Stars Make Rushing through the Sky* (2007).

OLIVE SCHREINER, 1855–1920

Olive Schreiner was born to a missionary couple in South Africa, receiving her early education from her mother and later at the school where her brother was headmaster. The family was avidly religious and lived in dire poverty. She questioned Christianity and eventually left home to be a governess, her experiences described in the acclaimed novel, *The Story of an African Farm* (1883), published under the name Ralph Iron, which for the first time made the landscape and people of southern Africa a reality for readers in England and America. In addition to its themes of religious crisis, colonialism, gender roles, and racism, it exhibited Modernist experimentation, overthrowing conventions of realism.

In 1894, she married farmer Samuel Cronwright, and the couple became active in politics, influential speakers on behalf of the Boer cause and in opposition to the capitalist exploitation of South Africa by British mining interests. Her critique of the situation was published as *An English South African Woman's View of the Situation* (1899).

Woman and Labor (1911) also revealed Schreiner's gifts as a polemicist, astutely demonstrating the dependent, parasitic nature of the woman's role in conventional marriage, and insisting on equal civic status and professional training for women. Her own marriage was strained and she separated from her husband in 1913, moving to London, where she lived in relative isolation during the war. She returned in 1920 to South Africa, where she died and is buried atop a mountain among the farms where she worked as a governess.

ROBERT LOUIS STEVENSON, 1850–1894

Prolific poet, travel writer, and novelist, Robert Louis Stevenson was a critically esteemed author in his day, and classics such as *Treasure Island* (1883), *A Child's Garden of Verses* (1885), *Kidnapped* (1886), *The Strange Case of Dr. Jekyll and Mr. Hyde* (1886), and *In the South Seas* (1896) continue to be popular.

An only child, sickly and odd, he was born into a Scottish family of lighthouse engineers on his father's side and of landed gentry on his mother's.

He was educated at private schools and by tutors during periods of illness, and ultimately read law at the University of Edinburgh. Although admitted to the bar in 1875, he never practiced law and began to break from his family, sporting bohemian dress, rejecting Christianity, and putting all his efforts into travel and writing, which met immediate praise. In 1880, he married Fanny Van de Grift Osbourne, who helped him reconcile with his parents.

Searching for a locale suitable to his frail health, the family resided in Scotland, England, France, and New York. In 1888, he embarked with his family on a voyage to the Pacific, visiting Hawaii, Tahiti, and Samoa, where he lived until his death, having assumed the indigenous name Tusitala ("storyteller"). His tomb, on a spot overlooking the sea, is inscribed with words from his poem, "Requiem": "Home is the sailor, home from the sea / And the hunter home from the hill."

JOHN MILLINGTON SYNGE, 1871–1909

John Millington Synge was a key figure in the Irish literary renaissance of the early twentieth century and a founder of the influential Abbey Theatre in Dublin. Born into an affluent Protestant family, he was educated at private schools and at the Royal Academy of Music—where he studied several instruments and musical theory—and at Trinity College. In addition to his talent for music, he was gifted with languages, including Gaelic, Hebrew, German, French, and Italian. He studied intensely the sonnets of Petrarch, and toward the end of his life translated seventeen of them.

While Synge's own poetry is considered of less value than his plays, the language of the plays is without a doubt poetic prose, lyrical and robust. He met Yeats in 1896, who found his poems lifeless and admonished him to go to the Aran Islands to live "as if you were one of the people themselves; express a life that has never found expression." Plays such as *In the Shadow of the Glen* (1903), *Riders to the Sea* (1904), *The Well of Saints* (1905), and *The Tinker's Wedding* (1908) each focus intimate attention on rural life, relishing the vigor of peasant language, revealing ironic wit and an epic talent for storytelling. But it was his masterpiece, *The Playboy of the Western World* (1907), that earned him a reputation as the most influential dramatist of the Irish revival, even though its first public performance caused a riot. Synge died of Hodgkin's disease and is buried in Dublin.

MARY THACHER [HIGGINSON], 1844–1941

Poet, biographer, and essayist, Mary Thacher Higginson was the second wife of Thomas Wentworth Higginson, an influential Unitarian minister, abolitionist, author, and mentor to Emily Dickinson. She is best remembered for her biography, *Thomas Wentworth Higginson: the Story of His Life* (1914), for editing *The Letters and Journals of Thomas Wentworth Higginson, 1846–1906* (1921), and for *The Playmate Hours* (1891), a collection of her poems.

CELIA THAXTER, 1835–1894

American author Celia Laighton Thaxter was raised on White Island, Isles of Shoals, New Hampshire, where her father was a lighthouse keeper. When she was twelve, her father built the first resort on the New England coast, Appledore House Hotel in Maine, which attracted literary and artistic luminaries such as Nathaniel Hawthorne, Harriet Beecher Stowe, Sarah Orne Jewett, and William Morris Hunt.

At age sixteen, she married her tutor and father's business partner, Levi Thaxter, and moved with him to the mainland, settling in Newtonville, Massachusetts, where she bore two sons. During this time her first poem, "Land-Locked" (1861), was published in the *Atlantic Monthly.* After ten years of fairly unharmonious marriage, Thaxter returned to Appledore, serving as hostess of the hotel, and creating her renowned gardens, immortalized in paintings by Childe Hassam and Ellen Robbins.

By the late nineteenth century, Thaxter had become one of America's favorite authors, known for poems such as "The Great White Owl," "The Kingfisher," and "The Sandpiper," and for her books, *Among the Isles of Shoals* (1873), *An Island Garden* (1894), and *Stories and Poems for Children* (1895).

HENRY DAVID THOREAU, 1817–1862

Henry David Thoreau—poet, essayist, ambler, and tax resister—gained more acclaim in the twentieth century than in his own day, his creed of simple living inspiring activists such as Gandhi and Martin Luther King, to say nothing of the mid-century Aquarian generation that yearned to march to "a different drummer" in the face of social upheaval. He was born to a genteel yet fairly impoverished family that eventually saw better days; he attended the public school in Concord and then Harvard College.

After graduation, he taught in fits and starts to support himself and became acquainted with Emerson, who introduced him to fellow

Transcendentalists and prominent literary figures, and provided a venue for publication in the *Dial*. It was Emerson who suggested to Thoreau that he keep a journal, launching the younger man on a course that lasted his entire lifetime. Ultimately, the journals filled forty volumes and became a cornerstone of American literature.

Thoreau's time sequestered in a cabin on Walden Pond began as a way of coping with the loss of his brother. There he determined to write an account of a row-boating trip they had taken, which became *A Week on the Concord and Merrimack Rivers* (1849). This was followed by the controversial "Civil Disobedience" (initially a lecture delivered in 1848), and his masterwork, *Walden* (1854), the timeless model for nature writing, a mordant critique of human foibles, and an early example of modern American prose.

EDITH WHARTON, 1862–1937

A master of fiction with a witty, clear vision of the upper classes of society, Edith Wharton and Henry James have been deemed "the tutelary and benign gods of our American literature." Her wealthy, conservative family provided her with every privilege—private education, international travel, fashion, and marriage to a well-heeled (albeit older and depressive) husband—and copious material for her books.

Although her first novel wasn't published until she was forty, Wharton's gifts were immediately recognized. Her first book of short stories, *The Greater Inclination* (1899), earned a nod from James, who detected in it echoes of George Eliot. With *Ethan Frome* (1911), she demonstrated keen craft in the novella form. Her principal theme, as described in *The Writing of Fiction* (1925), was the conflict between individual desire and social convention, reflecting many of her own struggles as a woman of wealth and position.

Her approach was to mine material she knew intimately and to discover the deeper significance in every character. Writing about the commercial aristocracy of Old New York—in best-selling novels such as *The House of Mirth* (1905) and *The Age of Innocence* (1920)—helped her realize that "a frivolous society can acquire dramatic significance only through what its frivolity destroys . . . debasing people and ideals." Wharton won the Pulitzer Prize in 1921, making her the first woman to win the award. She died in 1937 in France, where she had lived since 1906, and is buried at Versailles.

WALT WHITMAN, 1819–1892

"The best writing," said Walt Whitman, "has no lace on its sleeves." Proponent and practitioner of modern writing—intuitive, robust, sympathetic, direct, sensual—he was the prophet of the new democratic order, herald of a distinct American voice, and the poet of the transcendent self. Poet, critic, newspaperman, Whitman began life on Long Island and then Brooklyn, where he received his only formal education, six years in public schools. As a young man, he taught school, worked as a printer's devil, and edited and wrote for newspapers in the New York area. Newspaper work exposed him to the great writers of his time—Emerson, Poe, Thoreau, Bryant, Longfellow—and set him to reading European and Eastern classics.

Leaves of Grass (1855), which Emerson considered "the most extraordinary piece of wit and wisdom that America has yet contributed," consisted of a long prefatory manifesto and twelve untitled, free-verse poems, and underwent seven revised editions by the time of Whitman's death. His first widely-distributed book of prose, *Democratic Vistas* (1871), written during Reconstruction, despaired of the success of the American experiment in democracy, insisting upon the need for a reconciliation of individualism with brotherhood.

In his fifties, Whitman suffered a paralytic stroke and moved from Washington, D.C., to Camden, New Jersey, to live with his brother. *Two Rivulets* (1876) and *Specimen Days & Collect* (1882–1883) reissued early work, giving his literary criticism and journalism a broader audience now that he was famous. After his death, a public viewing of Whitman's body drew more than a thousand visitors to Camden to pay their respects.

OSCAR WILDE, 1854–1900

Known for his mordant wit and extravagant dress, Oscar Wilde was a man of contradiction, controversy, and extremes—and one of the best-known personalities of his day. He was born in Dublin to Anglo-Irish parents, learned French and German at an early age, and showed great promise as a classicist at Trinity College and Oxford, where he blossomed under the tutelage of Walter Pater and John Ruskin, philosophers of the budding field of aestheticism.

A master of many genres, he wrote poetry, fiction, criticism, epigrams, short stories, and plays. Among his enduring works are *The Happy Prince and Other Stories* (1888), *The Picture of Dorian Gray* (1891), *Lady Windemere's Fan* (1892), *Salome: A Tragedy in One Act* (1894), *An Ideal Husband* (1898), *The Importance of Being*

Earnest (1898), and "De Profundis" (1897).

A husband and father of two sons—one of whom died in the First World War—Wilde also had enduring intimate relationships with men, and was convicted in 1895 of gross indecency and sentenced to two years of imprisonment, after which he lived the remainder of his life in France. He is buried outside Paris, his tomb engraved with a verse from "The Ballad of Reading Gaol" (1898): "And alien tears will fill for him / Pity's long-broken urn, / For his mourners will be outcast men, / And outcasts always mourn."

In 2017, Wilde was posthumously pardoned, along with more than fifty thousand other gay men, for crimes of homosexuality that no longer exist.

MARY E. WILKINS [FREEMAN], 1852–1930

Mary Eleanor Wilkins was born to a strict, religious New England family, constraint providing one of the major themes in her work. The family's dry goods store failed in the financial panic of 1873; her mother died three years later and her father in 1883, leaving her impoverished. She turned to writing as a source of income, launching her career with the publication of "The Ghost Family" (1881). Over a lifetime, she wrote more than two dozen books, the most renowned being the short-story collections, *A New England Nun and Other Stories* (1891), *A Humble Romance and Other Stories* (1897), *The People of Our Neighborhood* (1898), and the novel, *Pembroke* (1894).

In 1902, she married Dr. Charles Manning Freeman, establishing her professional name as Mary E. Wilkins Freeman, and building a home in Metuchen, New Jersey. The marriage was short-lived, due to Freeman's infidelities and alcoholism, which landed him in a mental hospital. In April 1926, she was awarded the William Dean Howells medal for fiction from the American Academy of Arts and Letters, the first woman so honored. While her work has at times been characterized as local-color fiction, she sensitively dealt with Puritan heritage and village life in New England to such an extent that she is credited with a significant role in the development of realism in American literature.

ZITKÁLA-ŠÁ [GERTRUDE SIMMONS BONNIN], 1876–1938

Sioux writer, teacher, and activist, Zitkála-Šá left the Yankton Reservation in South Dakota at age eight to be educated at an assimilationist boarding school in Indiana and at Earlham College. A talented violinist, she also studied at the New England Conservatory of Music, and she later taught music at the Carlisle Indian School. Much of her writing examines the struggles of indigenous peoples living within a dominant culture that is hostile and exploitative. She felt that her status as a white-educated Indian put her "in the heart of chaos, beyond the touch or voice of human aid."

She married Raymond Bonnin, also a Yankton Sioux, and moved to the Uintah-Ouray Reservation in Utah, where they worked for fourteen years. She collaborated with composer William Hanson of Brigham Young University, writing the libretto for *The Sun Dance Opera*, produced in 1913 and featuring Ute performers. (The New York Light Opera Guild chose it in 1937 as the American opera of the year.)

Old Indian Legends, Retold by Zitkala-Sa (1902) and *American Indian Stories* (1921) introduced Native American culture to a broad American audience, as did articles like "An Indian Teaching Among Indians" (1900), "Soft-Hearted Sioux" (1901) and "Why I Am a Pagan" (1902), published in national magazines such as *Atlantic Monthly* and *Harper's Monthly*. In 1926, she founded the National Council of American Indians and served as its president until her death. She is buried in Arlington National Cemetery.

Bibliographic Notes

INTRODUCTION

[1] Edgar Allan Poe, "The Philosophy of Composition," *The Works of Edgar Allan Poe*, ed. E. C. Stedman and G. E. Woodberry, 10 vols. (New York: Scribner's, 1914), 6:34; first published in *Graham's Magazine* (April 1856). Robert Alexander, "Afterword: Supple and Jarring," *Family Portrait: American Prose Poetry, 1900–1950* (Buffalo, NY: White Pine Press, 2012), 239.

[2] Lafcadio Hearn, "The Prose of Small Things," *Life and Literature*, ed. John Erskine (New York: Dodd Mead, 1917), 113–114. This is a third selection from lectures delivered at the University of Tokyo between 1896 and 1902; the other two volumes are *Interpretations of Literature* (1915) and *Appreciations of Poetry* (1916).

[3] In fact, chapbooks constituted the bulk of popular literature up until the eighteenth century. For an excellent discussion of this species of publication, see John Ashton, "Chap-books," *The Chap-Book*, vol. 3, no. 1 (May 15, 1895), 3–13. Many early examples can be seen in *A Hundred Merry Tales and Other English Jestbooks of the Fifteenth and Sixteenth Century*, ed. P. M. Zall (Lincoln: Univ. of Nebraska Press, 1963): "their style is conversationally dramatic, vernacular vs. literary, and sometimes seemingly taken down from actual speech" [Introduction, p. 2]. Samuel Pepys was a great collector of such items, which have been reproduced in *Samuel Pepys' Penny Merriments: Being a Collection of Chapbooks, Full of Histories, Jests, Magic, Amorous Tales of Courtship, Marriage and Infidelity, Accounts of Rogues and Fools, Together with Comments on the Times*, ed. Roger Thompson (New York: Columbia Univ. Press, 1977).

[4] Charles Baudelaire, "À Arsène Houssaye," dedicatory letter in *Petits Poèmes en prose (Le Spleen de Paris)*, ed. Henri Lemaître (Paris: Garnier, 1962), 6–7 [first published 1869]; translated by the author, who is indebted to Raymond Mackenzie for the use of "jarring" for *heurtée*. For the excerpt from Baudelaire's journal in which he credits Alphonse Rabbe, see Pierre Moreau, "La tradition Française du poème en prose avant Baudelaire," *Archives des lettre modernes*, vol. 3, no. 19/20 (Jan.–Feb. 1959), 26. For the history of the prose poem in France, see Mary Ann Caws and Hermine B. Rifaterre, eds., *The Prose Poem in France: Theory and Practice* (New York: Columbia Univ. Press, 1983); also Suzanne

Bernard, *Le Poème en prose de Baudelaire jusqu'à nos jours* (Paris: Nizet, 1959). For a magisterial treatment of the prose poem in both English and French, see Steven Monte, *Invisible Fences: Prose Poetry as a Genre in French and American Literature* (Lincoln: Univ. of Nebraska Press, 2000).

[5] Lafcadio Hearn, "Spring Phantoms," *Fantastics and Other Fancies*, ed. Charles Woodward Hutson (Boston: Houghton Mifflin, 1919), 147–151. James Huneker, trans., *The Poems and Prose Poems of Charles Baudelaire* (New York: Brentano's, 1919). William Dean Howells, "The Prose Poem," introduction to *Pastels in Prose*, ed. and trans. Stuart Merrill (New York: Harper & Brothers, 1890), v, vii. In its unsigned review of *Pastels in Prose*—headlined "A Dainty Volume"—the *New York Times* had this to say: "You cannot take 'Pastels in Prose' and read it appreciatively by beginning at Page 1 and running through it to the finis. It has to be sipped with little tastings. Then the bouquet of it comes out" (April 13, 1890). The same could, I suspect, be said of this collection.

[6] Aloysuis [Louis] Bertrand, "Moonlight," trans. Stuart Merrill, *Pastels in Prose*, 11– 12.

[7] Charles Baudelaire, "The Gifts of the Moon," trans. James Huneker, *The Poems and Prose Poems of Charles Baudelaire* (New York: Brentano's, 1919), 97–98.

SPRING PHANTOMS

[1] William Blake, *The Marriage of Heaven and Hell* [1790], in David V. Erdman, ed., *The Complete Poetry and Prose of William Blake*, Newly Revised Edition (Berkeley: Univ. of California Press, 1982), 35, 38–39, 40. For the original plates, see William Blake, *The Marriage of Heaven and Hell*, "reproduction in the original size of William Blake's Illuminated Book, with introduction and commentary by Sir Geoffrey Keynes" (Oxford: Oxford Univ. Press, 1975), plates 6–7, 12–13, 15. Swinburne says that it is "the greatest of all his books; a work indeed which we rank as about the greatest produced by the eighteenth century in the line of high poetry and spiritual speculation." It is, according to Swinburne, "the high-water mark of his intellect. . . . [H]ere for once he has written a book as perfect as his most faultless song, as great as his most imperfect rhapsody. His fire of spirit fills it from end to end; but never deforms the body, never singes the surface of the work, as too often in the still noble books of his later life" [Algernon Charles Swinburne, *William Blake: A Critical Essay* (London, 1868), 204–205].

[2] Leigh Hunt, "A 'Now,' Descriptive of a Hot Day," *Essays by Leigh Hunt*, ed.

with intro. and notes by Arthur Symons (London: Walter Scott, 1887), 59–61; originally published in *The Indicator* (1820). In one anthology, a brief statement by Hunt precedes this piece, taken from his *Autobiography*, chapter 16: "The paper that was most liked by Keats, if I remember, was the one on a hot summer's day, entitled *A Now*. He was with me when I was writing and reading it to him, and contributed one or two of the passages" [Russell Noyes, ed., *English Romantic Poetry and Prose* (New York: Oxford Univ. Press, 1956), 766–767]; the page notes are from this same source.

[3] Henry R. Schoolcraft [and Jane Johnston Schoolcraft], trans. and comp., "Peeta Kway, The Foam-Woman, An Ottawa Legend" and "Leelinau, A Chippewa Tale," *The Myth of Hiawatha and Other Oral Legends, Mythologic and Allegoric, of the North American Indians* (Philadelphia: Lippincott, 1856), 213–215, 299–301. The page notes are Schoolcraft's. Though he doesn't give his wife credit as translator or compiler, she was an essential partner in his research and translation. The daughter of the fur trader John Johnston (1762–1828) and Ozhaawashkodewekwe (Woman of the Green Glade [c. 1775 – c. 1840]), her own writing can be found in Robert Dale Parker, ed., *The Sound the Stars Make Rushing through the Sky: The Writings of Jane Johnston Schoolcraft* (Philadelphia: Univ. of Pennsylvania Press, 2007).

[4] [Richard Horne], "The Old Churchyard Tree: A Prose Poem," *Pearl-Fishing: Choice Stories from Dickens' Household Words*, First Series (Auburn [N.Y.]: Alden, Beardsley, 1854), 173–178. This piece first appeared, without attribution (as it is in *Pearl Fishing*), in *Household Words: A Weekly Journal Conducted by Charles Dickens*, vol. 1, no. 16 (July 13, 1850), 377–378. It was reprinted "across the pond" in *Harper's New Monthly Magazine*, vol. 1, no. 4 (Sept. 1850), 483, where the only credit given is as follows: "From Dickens's *Household Words*"). Attribution for this piece can be found on Dickens Journals Online: http://www.djo.org.uk/indexes/articles/chips-the-old-churchyard-tree-a-prose- poem.html. It is attributed there to Horne and an "unknown" author, but my opinion is that this refers to the particular section entitled "Chips" in which it appears as one of several separate pieces. In fact, "Chips" appears in ten different places in that first volume of *Household Words*, containing letters to the editor and other unattributed, short prose pieces.

[5] Ralph Waldo Emerson, "Woods: A Prose Sonnet," *The Journals and Miscellaneous Notebooks of Ralph Waldo Emerson*, ed. A. W. Plumstead and Harrison Hayford (Campbridge, MA: Belknap Press, 1969), 248; written in 1839.

[6] Nathaniel Hawthorne, "Sketches from Memory, No. 2," *The New-England*

Magazine, vol. 9, no. 11 (December 1835), 408–409; published anonymously under the byline "A Pedestrian"; reprinted in *Hawthorne's American Travel Sketches,* ed. Alfred Weber, Beth L. Lueck, and Dennis Berthold (Hanover, NH: Univ. Press of New England, 1989), 47–49. "August 31, 1836," *Passages from the American Notebooks,* 2 vols. (Boston, 1884), 1:28–29. "Autumnal Characteristics," *American Notebooks,* ed. Claude M. Simpson (Columbus: Ohio State Univ. Press, 1972), 554– 555; a single leaf by Hawthorne apparently written for a collector, or perhaps for an auction. Except for the last sentence, the entire piece is lifted from two entries in the *Notebooks* (October 14 and 16, 1837). There are places where Hawthorne has either condensed or expanded the text from which the paragraph is constructed, but the last sentence has no counterpart. Other than that one sentence, Hawthorne merely dressed up observations and details that he'd noted in his journal. But when it came to the final statement, he presumably felt he had to do more. Why? In all likelihood, he wasn't content to leave the piece seeming "merely" like a passage from his notebooks—and so he created the last sentence with its intimation of mortality.

[7] Edgar Allan Poe, "Shadow—A Parable," *Poems and Tales,* Volume 2 of *The Works of the Late Edgar Allan Poe,* 4 vols. (New York: Blakeman & Mason, 1859), 292– 294.

[8] [Harriet Jacobs], *Incidents in the Life of a Slave Girl, Written by Herself,* ed. L[ydia] Maria Child (Boston: Published for the Author, 1861), 25–27, 67–70, 179–182, 264– 267. For more information about the remarkable life of this remarkable woman, see www.harrietjacobs.org.

[9] Henry David Thoreau, "Aug. 18," *Journal,* vol. 5, ed. Bradford Torrey (Boston: Houghton Mifflin, 1906), 378–379. "September 9th, 1857," *Faith in a Seed: The Dispersion of Seeds, and Other Late Natural History Writings,* ed. Bradley P. Dean (Washington, DC: Island Press, 1993), 39. "Walking," *Atlantic Monthly,* vol. 9, no. 56 (June 1862), 673–674; this essay (pp. 657–674) is a sequence of shorter pieces set apart by spaces—included here are two of those pieces, which appear in the same order in the original; reprinted in *Henry David Thoreau, Excursions* (Boston: Ticknor & Fields, 1863), 161–214.

[10] *Walt Whitman, Specimen Days & Collect* (Philadelphia: David McKay, 1882–'83), 43–44, 45–46, 80–81, 88, 159. Starting in 1862 as a volunteer in army hospitals during the Civil War, Whitman kept detailed notes, sketches he published in 1875 as *Memoranda during the War,* and which he later included in *Specimen Days;* his plan for the "middle of the book," as he says, "was originally for hints and data of a Nature-poem that should carry one's experience a few hours,

commencing at noon-flush, and so through the after-part of the day—I suppose led to such idea by own life's afternoon having arrived" [*Specimen Days,* p. 199].

[11] Jourdon Anderson, "Letter from a Freedman to His Old Master," *The Freeedmen's Book,* ed. L[ydia] Maria Child (Boston: Ticknor & Fields, 1866), 265–267; "written just as he dictated it." Published in the *New York Daily Tribune,* Aug. 22, 1865, reprinted from the *Cincinnati Commercial.*

[12] Dante Gabriel Rossetti, "The Cup of Water" and "Michael Scott's Wooing," in "Stories and Schemes of Poems," *The Collected Works of Dante Gabriel Rossetti,* ed. with preface and notes by William M. Rossetti, 2 vols. (London: Ellis & Scrutton, 1886), 1:437–440.

[13] Mary Mapes Dodge, "Our Vegetables," *Harper's New Monthly Magazine,* vol. 33, no. 196 (September 1866), 523–524. "Migratory Husbands," *Theophilus and Others* (New York: Scribner, Armstrong, 1876), 213–215.

[14] Ada Clare [Jane McElhenney], "The Slave of the House," *Vanity Fair,* vol. 1, no. 2 (January 14, 1860), 43. For an intriguing personal memoir, see Charles Warren Stoddard, "Ada Clare, Queen of Bohemia," *The National Magazine,* vol. 22, no. 6 (Sept. 1905), 637–645.

[15] Celia Thaxter, *An Island Garden* (Boston: Houghton Mifflin, 1894), 54–60; these pieces appear here as in the book, with no intervening material.

[16] Elizabeth Stuart Phelps, "How Shall Women Dress?" *The North American Review,* vol. 140, no. 343 (June 1885), 564. This brief essay was part of a forum discussion, pp. 557–572, with contributions by E. M. King, Charles Dudley Warner, William A. Hammond, and Kate J. Jackson.

[17] Mary P. Thacher [Higginson], "Passenger Pigeons," *Seashore and Prairie* (Boston: James R. Osgood, 1877), 89–93. Compare this description by Audubon: "In the autumn of 1813, I left my house at Henderson, on the banks of the Ohio, on my way to Louisville. In passing over the Barrens a few miles beyond Hardensburgh, I observed the pigeons flying from north-east to south-west, in greater numbers than I thought I had ever seen them before, and feeling an inclination to count the flocks that might pass within the reach of my eye in one hour, I dismounted, seated myself on an eminence, and began to mark with my pencil, making a dot for every flock that passed. In a short time finding the task which I had undertaken impracticable, as the birds poured in in countless multitudes, I rose, and counting the dots then put down, found that 163 had been made in twenty-one minutes. I travelled on, and still met more the farther I proceeded. The air was literally filled

with Pigeons; the light of noon-day was obscured as by an eclipse; the dung fell in spots, not unlike melting flakes of snow; and the continued buzz of wings had a tendency to lull my senses to repose.

"Whilst waiting for dinner at Young's inn, at the confluence of Salt-River with the Ohio, I saw, at my leisure, immense legions still going by, with a front reaching far beyond the Ohio on the west, and the beech-wood forests directly on the east of me. . . . I cannot describe to you the extreme beauty of their aerial evolutions, when a Hawk chanced to press upon the rear of a flock. At once, like a torrent, and with a noise like thunder, they rushed into a compact mass, pressing upon each other towards the centre. In these almost solid masses, they darted forward in undulating and angular lines, descended and swept close over the earth with inconceivable velocity, mounted perpendicularly so as to resemble a vast column, and, when high, were seen wheeling and twisting within their continued lines, which then resembled the coils of a gigantic serpent.

"Before sunset I reached Louisville, distant from Hardensburgh fifty-five miles. The Pigeons were still passing in undiminished numbers, and continued to do so for three days in succession" [John James Audubon, "The Passenger Pigeon," *Ornithological Biography*, vol. 1 (Philadelphia, 1832), 320–321].

[18] Emma Lazarus, "By the Waters of Babylon: Little Poems in Prose," *The Century*, vol. 33, no. 5 (March 1887), 801–803.

[19] Kate Chopin, "Ripe Figs," "An Idle Fellow," "The Story of an Hour," and "The Night Came Slowly," *The Complete Works of Kate Chopin*, 2 vols., ed. Per Seyerstad (Baton Rouge: Lousiana State Univ. Press, 1997), 1:199, 280–281, 352–354, 366; bibliographic information can be found in vol. 2, 1003–1032. "Ripe Figs" was written on Feb. 26, 1892, and was first published in *Vogue* (Aug. 19, 1893); "An Idle Fellow" was written on June 9, 1893, but not published until it appeared in the *Complete Works*; "The Story of an Hour" was written on April 19, 1894, and first appeared in *Vogue* (Dec. 6, 1894); and "The Night Came Slowly" was written on July 24, 1894, and was first published in *Moods: A Journal Intime* (July, 1895).

[20] Lafcadio Hearn, "The Stranger" and "Spring Phantoms," *Fantastics and Other Fancies*, ed. Charles Woodward Hutson (Boston: Houghton Mifflin, 1919), 51–53, 147–151; both pieces first appeared in the *New Orleans Item:* April 17, 1880, and April 21, 1881. Hutson's note indicates that "Spring Phantoms" was Hearn's own title (*Fantastics*, p. 147).

[21] Robert Louis Stevenson, "Fables," *Letters and Miscellanies of Robert Louis Stevenson*

(New York: Scribner's, 1896), 455–456, 476–477, 478.

[22] Grace King, "The Balcony," *The Century*, vol. 45, no. 2 (Dec. 1892), 279–280; reprinted in *Balcony Stories* (New York: The Century Co., 1893), 1–4.

[23] Mary E. Wilkins [Freeman], "Pastels in Prose," *Harper's New Monthly Magazine*, vol. 86, no. 511 (December 1892), 147–148.

[24] Oscar Wilde, "The Artist," "The Doer of Good," and "The Disciple," *Poems in Prose*, vol. 9 of *The Works of Oscar Wilde* (New York: Lamb, 1909), 9–10, 11–13, 15–16.

[25] Olive Schreiner, *Dreams*, Second Edition (London: T. Fisher Unwin, 1891), 53–55, 115–116, 119–121.

[26] Fiona Macleod [William Sharp], "The Silence of Amor," *From the Hills of Dream: Mountain Songs and Island Runes* (Edinburgh: Patrick Geddes, [1897]), 127, 129, 133, 146.

[27] Alcée Fortier, ed., "The Tortoise [Tortie]" and "The Devil's Marriage [Mariaze Djabe]," *Lousiana Folk-Tales: In French Dialect and English Translation* (Boston: Houghton Mifflin, 1895), 29, 69–75. Note for "The Tortoise" [p.95]: "This is an amusing story, and it shows that the tortoise deserves to share with the fox and the rabbit the reputation of being the most cunning animals. . . . Informant, Julia, 7 Prytania Street, New Orleans." Note for "The Devil's Marriage: [p. 96]: "The incident of the obstacles thrown in the way of the pursuer are common to many stories. M. Cosquin gives 'Le Sifflet Enchante,' 'L'Oiseau Vert,' 'La Chatte Blanche,' 'Le Prince et son Cheval,' in which are found some of the incidents of the 'Devil's Marriage.' The warning of the old woman to take dirty eggs and not clean ones belongs essentially to folklore, and the women hanging in the closet is a motive of the Blue Beard type. Climbing up the pole to catch the pumpkin has a local color peculiar to Louisiana, and the ingratitude to the old horse is another incident often found in folk-tales. Informant, old negro at *la Vacherie*." "The Tortoise," it will be noticed, runs well over a thousand words, but as it is presented in short segments, I felt it was reasonable to include it in this collection.

[28] James Gibbons Huneker, ["Nuptials Royal"], *Steeplejack*, Two Volumes in One (New York: Scribner's, 1920), 2:194–195; as Huneker notes in introducing this piece, "I wrote many, so-called prose-poems, seduced by the examples of Baudelaire, Mallarmé, and Huysmans. . . . Here is one, never before reprinted, from *M'lle New York*." Though Huneker presents it in *Steeplejack* without a title (and slightly edited), the original is called "Nuptials Royal" in *M'lle*

New York, New Series, vol. 2, no. 1 (Nov. 1898), n.p.; at that time, Huneker was the associate editor of the magazine.

[29] Mary Alicia Owen, ed., "How the Skunk Became the Terror of All Living Creatures—A Short Chapter furnished by Big Angy," *Ole Rabbit's Plantation Stories, as told Among the Negroes of the Southwest: Collected from Original Sources* (Philadelphia: George W. Jacobs, 1898), 190–192.

[30] Charlotte Perkins Gilman, "An Extinct Angel" and "Deserted," *The Yellow Wall-Paper and Other Stories,* ed. Robert Shulman (Oxford, UK: Oxford Univ. Press, 1995), 48–50, 62–65. "An Extinct Angel" first appeared in *Kate Field's Washington* (23 September 1890), 199–200; "Deserted" first appeared in the *San Francisco Call* (10 July 1893), 1–2. "Prisons for Animals" is printed on a sheet tipped into the inside of the cover of a bound first volume of her magazine, *The Forerunner* 1, no. 1 (November 1909)—specifically, the copy in the Stanford University Library (barcode #105005437921); on the facing page is an ex libris sticker showing that it was the bequest of Dr. Clelia Mosher. At the bottom of the single sheet is the following credit: "Western Press Committee, 611 Gilman Street, Palo Alto, California," with a colophon that appears to be a union logo. All the ellipses are included in the original.

[31] Edith Wharton, "The Valley of Childish Things, and Other Emblems," *The Century* 52, no. 3 (July 1896), 467–469; reprinted in *The Collected Short Stories of Edith Wharton,* ed. R. W. B. Lewis, 2 vols. (New York: Scribner, 1968), 1:58–63.

[32] Florence Merriam, *Birds through an Opera Glass* (Boston: Houghton Mifflin, 1889), 18–20, 144–145.

[33] Robert W. Chambers, "The Prophet's Paradise," *The King in Yellow* (New York: Harper & Brothers, 1902), 123–124, 126, 128, 130.

[34] Bruce Porter, "The Return of Spring," *The Lark,* no. 13 (May 1896), n.p.

[35] Gelett Burgess, "The Adjective Family," *The Lark,* no. 8 (Dec. 1895), n.p.; "The Mutual Advice Association," *The Lark,* no. 9 (December 1896), n.p.; "The Confessions of a Yellster," *The Lark,* no. 22 (Feb. 1897), n.p.

[36] Ernest Dowson, "Absinthia Taetra," "The Visit," and "The Princess of Dreams," *Decorations: In Verse and Prose* (London: Leonard Smithers, 1899), 46, 47–48, 49– 50.

[37] Stephen Crane, "How the Donkey Lifted the Hills," "The Judgment of the Sage," and "The Seaside Hotel Hop," *Tales, Sketches, and Reports,* ed. Fredson Bowers (Charlottesville: Univ. Press of Virginia, 1973), 91–94, 98–99, 527–528. "How the Donkey Lifted the Hills" first appeared in the *Nebraska State*

Journal (June 6, 1895), p. 4; "The Judgment of the Sage" first appeared in *The Bookman*, vol. 2 (January 1896), 412; and "The Seaside Hotel Hop" first appeared in the *New York Tribune* (September 11, 1892), p. 15, with the full title, "The Seaside Hotel Hop: An Institution that Flourishes Mildly in Certain Neighborhoods.".

[38] John Millington Synge, "Translations from Petrarach: Sonnets from 'Laura in Death,' " *Poems and Translations* (Dublin: Maunsel, 1911), 31, 32, 35, 40; originally published in 1909 by Cuala Press. "The highest praise these translations have received, ironically, came from C. S. Lewis, who, in the midst of a discussion of Renaissance Petrarchism, the thrust of which was to distinguish Petrarch from his later imitators, made this telling aside: 'Readers who do not know Italian will, by the way, learn much more of that strange great work [Petrarch's *Rime*] from Synge's prose version than from all the Elizabethans and all the Pléiade put together' (C. S. Lewis, *English Literature in the Sixteenth Century excluding Drama* [Oxford,1954], p. 229). I think Synge's translations are more influenced by Renaissance Petrarchism than Lewis implies here, but Lewis's assessment of the faithfulness of Synge's translations is high praise indeed, coming from a great medieval and Renaissance scholar" [Reed Way Dasenbrock, "Synge's Irish Renaissance Petrarchism," *Modern Philology*, vol. 83, no. 1 (Aug. 1985), 33–44; this particular quote can be found on p. 33 fn 1]. The whole article, which focuses on Synge's translations from Petrarch's sonnets, is well worth reading.

[39] H[arrison] G[arfield] R[hodes], "Sketches," *The Chap-Book*, vol. 1, no. 10 (Oct 1, 1894), 259–260. Rhodes was assistant editor of the magazine.

[40] Dora Greenwell McChesney, "At Old Italian Casements," *The Yellow Book*, vol. 13 (April 1897), 144–148.

[41] Max Beerbohm, "A Good Prince," *The Savoy*, no. 1 (January 1896), 45–47; reprinted in *The Works of Max Beerbohn*, with a biography by John Lane (New York: Dodd Mead, 1922), 35–39.

[42] S. P. Carrick, Jr., "A Geological Parable," *The Fly Leaf*, vol. 1, no. 2 (January 1896), 9. *The Fly Leaf* was one of the many little magazines—or "bibelots," as they were called at the time—published during the 1890s (*The Lark* and the *Chap-Book* being two others that are represented in this anthology). Published in Boston and edited by Walter Blackburn Harte, *The Fly Leaf* had as its subtitle, "A Pamphlet Periodical of the New—the new man, new woman, new ideas, whimsies and things." In the same issue as appeared Carrick's piece, there was an unsigned editorial giving the credo of the magazine, which may

be said to have applied to the whole rash of such publications: "There is a revolt and a quickening sense of changes and forces in the air. . . . When we say we appeal to the younger people it must not be thought that we appeal to the children—although since they are so far more critical than their grandparents, we shall not dare to forget them altogether. We mean that we desire to enlist the interests and sympathies of our own generation—say those born sometime in the sixties and since. Our grandparents may be very good folk and quite smart in getting around today, but they were largely brought up on almanacs, and their literary tastes are narrow and eccentric without being picturesque. They belong to ancient times without holding the antique novelties of the really far away ancient times, which were really more in touch with the intellectual bustle and eager curiosity of our day than those gray years of smug Anglo-Saxon absorption in a civilization of mere bread and beer that lie immediately behind us, and still cast the chill shadow of their prurient morality over all our literature. Even some of the direct parents of this generation are a little threadbare in their craniums. They have read domestic literature all their lives and of course are incapable of thought. The stirring gray matter is found in the heads of those born not much further back, say, than '49, the year of gold. Let us resolve to make this *fin de siècle* the golden age of American literature" ["The Vision of Youth," *The Fly Leaf*, vol. 1, no. 2 (Jan. 1896), 5–7].

[43] Yone Noguchi, *The Summer Cloud: Prose Poems* (Tokyo: Shunyodo, 1905), 20–21, 41–42, 92–93.

[44] Zitkála-Šá [Gertrude Simmons Bonnin], "Impressions of an Indian Childhood," *The Atlantic Monthly*, vol. 85, no. 507 (Jan. 1900), 37–38, 43–45; reprinted in *American Indian Stories* (Washington, DC: Hayworth Publishing House, 1912), 7–11, 30–38. For a further selection of her writing, see Zitkála-Šá, *Dreams and Thunder: Stories, Poems, and The Sun Dance Opera,* ed. P. Jane Hafen (Lincoln: Univ. of Nebraska Press, 2001).

[45] Lord Dunsany [Edward Plunkett], *Time and the Gods* (London: Heinemann, 1906), 81–84, 85–87.

THE MARIE ALEXANDER POETRY SERIES

Founded in 1996 by Robert Alexander, the Marie Alexander Poetry Series is dedicated to promoting the appreciation, enjoyment, and understanding of American prose poetry. Currently an imprint of White Pine Press, the series publishes one to two books annually. These are typically single-author collections of short prose pieces, sometimes interwoven with lineated sections, and an occasional anthology demonstrating the historical or international context within which American poetry exists. It is our mission to publish the very best contemporary prose poetry and to carry the rich tradition of this hybrid form on into the 21st century.

Series Editor: Robert Alexander
Editor: Nickole Brown

Volume 22
Spring Phantoms
Edited by Robert Alexander

Volume 21
Bright Advent
Robert Strong

Volume 20
Nothing to Declare: A Guide to the Flash Sequence
Edited by Robert Alexander, Eric Braun & Debra Marquart

Volume 19
To Some Women I Have Known
Re'Lynn Hansen

Volume 18
The Rusted City
Rochelle Hurt

Volume 17
Postage Due
Julie Marie Wade

Volume 16
Family Portrait: American Prose Poetry 1900–1950
Edited by Robert Alexander

Volume 15
All of Us
Elisabeth Frost

Volume 14
Angles of Approach
Holly Iglesias

Volume 13
Pretty
Kim Chinquee

Volume 12
Reaching Out to the World
Robert Bly

Volume 11
The House of Your Dream:
An International Collection of Prose Poetry
Edited by Robert Alexander and Dennis Maloney

Volume 10
Magdalena
Maureen Gibbon

Volume 9
The Angel of Duluth
Madelon Sprengnether

Volume 8
Light from an Eclipse
Nancy Lagomarsino

Volume 7
A Handbook for Writers
Vern Rutsala

Volume 6
The Blue Dress
Alison Townsend

Volume 5
Moments without Names: New & Selected Prose Poems
Morton Marcus

Volume 4
Whatever Shines
Kathleen McGookey

Volume 3
Northern Latitudes
Lawrence Millman

Volume 2
Your Sun, Manny
Marie Harris

Volume 1
Traffic
Jack Anderson